Overcoming Stagnation in Aid-Dependent Countries

CENTER FOR GLOBAL DEVELOPMENT

Overcoming Stagnation in Aid-Dependent Countries

Nicolas van de Walle

Washington, DC
March 2005

Nicolas van de Walle, nonresident fellow at the Center for Global Development, is the Jack S. Knight Professor of International Studies and director of the Mario Einaudi Center for International Studies at Cornell University. He has published widely on democratization issues as well as the politics of economic reform in Africa and the effectiveness of foreign aid. He has also advised international and multilateral organizations, including the World Bank, USAID, and the United Nations Development Program. He is the author or editor of seven books, including *African Economies and the Politics of Permanent Crisis, 1979–1999* (2001).

CENTER FOR GLOBAL DEVELOPMENT
1776 Massachusetts Avenue, NW, Suite 301
Washington, DC 20036
(202) 416-0700   FAX: (202) 416-0750

Nancy Birdsall, *President*

Typesetting by Sandra F. Watts
Printing by United Book Press, Inc.

Printed in the United States of America
07 06 05   5 4 3 2 1

Library of Congress Cataloging-in-Publication Data

van de Walle, Nicolas, 1957–
    Overcoming stagnation in aid-dependent countries / Nicolas van de Walle.
        p. cm.
    Includes bibliographical references and index.
    ISBN 1-933286-01-6
    1. Economic assistance—Developing countries.   2. Developing countries—Economic policy.   3. Developing countries—Foreign economic relations. I. Title.

HC60.V3427   2004
338.91'09172'4—dc22   2004056638

The views expressed in this publication are those of the author. This publication is part of the overall program of the Center, as endorsed by its Board of Directors, but does not necessarily reflect the views of individual members of the Board or the Advisory Committee.

Contents

Tables

Figures

Preface

A central feature of the international landscape for the last several decades has been the absence of economic growth in many of the poorest states of the world. With the significant exceptions of India and China, the economies of most countries that were poor three decades ago have grown little since. There is a sense in which globalization itself is leaving them behind. Meanwhile in the development community there is a crisis of confidence about the ability to help. Whether and how the rich world can make a difference in the poorest countries of Africa, Central Asia, and even Central America is a major global challenge and one to which the Center for Global Development devotes much of its attention.

In this book, Nicolas van de Walle identifies 26 countries that are extremely poor and grew little if at all in the 1990s. His sample excludes North Korea and countries where civil war explains some of their failure to grow (Afghanistan, Sierra Leone, Sudan, Tajikistan, and others). The 26 countries have limited infrastructure and human capital, and the small size of their markets deters private savings and investment. Aid was meant to help overcome these problems, and these countries received a lot. Yet they have failed to grow. What is wrong? Is foreign aid a solution or part of the problem? What changes might make aid more effective? Given these countries require the financial and technical resources of the West, why haven't aid programs made a difference?

Van de Walle blames the economic failure of these countries mostly on the venality and incompetence of their political leadership. He analyzes the contradictions and tensions faced by the aid community in poorly run countries, providing a sobering analysis of the perverse effects of aid where the politics is all wrong. Too often, resources provided by foreign aid keep incompetent or corrupt governments in office and undermine adoption of economic and political reforms. Aid combines with bad government to hurt poor countries—and particularly the poorest people in those countries. And despite good intentions, little progress has been made in implementing announced reforms of the aid business itself. A constituency for reform is lacking, not only in donor but in recipient countries, where those in power benefit from the status quo.

This is a book that everyone in the development business needs to read. It closes with a set of proposals for aid donors grounded in compelling and frank analysis of the problem. Van de Walle argues that foreign aid can play a positive role, but only if donors come to grips with the politics and incentives that currently prevail in the poorest countries. The business of aid is a risky and challenging one. The official aid community needs the will and the energy to take up a tough challenge. I and my colleagues at the Center for Global Development hope the evidence and the analysis herein add to the momentum for aid reform.

NANCY BIRDSALL
President

* * *

The Center for Global Development is an independent, nonprofit policy research organization dedicated to reducing global poverty and inequality and to making globalization work for the poor. Through a combination of research and strategic outreach, the Center actively engages policymakers and the public to influence the policies of the United States, other rich countries, and such institutions as the World Bank, the IMF, and the World Trade Organization (WTO), to improve the economic and social development prospects in poor countries. The Center's Board of Directors bears overall responsibility for the Center and includes distinguished leaders of nongovernmental organizations, former officials, business executives, and some of the world's leading scholars of development. The Center receives advice on its research and policy programs from the Board and from an Advisory Committee that comprises respected development specialists and advocates.

The Center's president works with the Board, the Advisory Committee, and the Center's senior staff in setting the research and program priorities and approves all formal publications. The Center is supported by an initial significant financial contribution from Edward W. Scott Jr. and by funding from philanthropic foundations and other organizations.

Acknowledgments

I wish to thank Nancy Birdsall and the staff of the Center for Global Development (CGD) for their help and patience as I wrote this book. Madona Devasahayam did a great job editing and often improving my prose. Noora-Lisa Aberman, Sheila Herrling, Lawrence McDonald, and Valerie Norville also deserve my thanks for ably shepherding my manuscript to publication. I am grateful to the participants of two CGD seminars, who greatly helped me sharpen my thinking on the main issues. I have also benefited from invaluable comments on previous drafts from a large number of friends and colleagues. I wish to offer my heartfelt thanks to Joel Barkan, Deborah Bräutigam, Bill Easterly, Milt Esman, John Gerring, Art Goldsmith, Catherine Gwin, Carol Lancaster, Kevin Morrison, Todd Moss, David Roodman, Joe Siegle, Alice Sindzingre, Mike Stevens, and Norman Uphoff. They definitely did not always agree with either my arguments or my conclusions, but their comments, encouragement and criticism improved this book immeasurably. Any remaining flaws are entirely of my own doing.

1

Introduction

In a famous 1988 essay, economist Robert Lucas suggested that the inability of the poorest economies of the world to grow was the most interesting intellectual puzzle facing modern economics. Given a world of capital mobility and international trade, traditional economic growth theory predicts the world's national economies will all eventually converge at the same level of income. Capital will flow to the poorer economies, where it is scarcer, and thus should find higher returns. As a result, developed economies should face reduced investment flows and grow more slowly, while the poorer countries benefit from a large flow of investment and grow faster. Theory predicts that inevitably the poorer countries catch up to the richest, and there is a convergence of the world's economies. Yet, as Lant Pritchett (1997) has put it, far from convergence, over the last half-century, the world economy has presented us with "divergence, big time." With a small number of exceptions, the poorest economies have not grown faster than the richest and do not appear to be catching up. In fact, some of the poorest countries have fallen further behind during the last couple of decades.

Why is this and what can be done about it? For 50 years, foreign aid has been the central policy instrument with which the international community has promoted economic development. The main justification for aid has always been that the poorest countries could not develop without it. Theories of economic development in the 1950s and 1960s viewed low-income countries as trapped in a low-level equilibrium, which they would not escape without external assistance. That the external impulse of financial and technical assistance could and should play a critical role in development has been a public policy adage that sustained growing volumes of aid from the end of World War II to the early 1990s. Yet, despite a large volume of aid and some striking individual aid success stories, a core set of the poorest countries has known little improvement in poverty rates, little or no economic growth, and a consistently poor governance record. A well-known paradox about aid has become that it tends to work best in the countries that need it least. For all its successes, aid has appeared to be the least successful in the poorest economies, where the needs are greatest.

The international aid community's failure to promote economic development in the poorest states of the developing world has shaken the policy community and led to something of a crisis of faith about foreign aid during the 1990s. A number of papers, books, and reports raised serious doubts about aid effectiveness.[1] While it rarely denied that aid had achieved many successes, this literature pointed to numerous flaws in aid design and implementation and called into doubt the ability of foreign aid to engineer the development of the poorest countries without substantial reform. Too often, large amounts of aid had been provided to incompetent dictators with wrong-headed economic policies. Some critics argued that aid was actually delaying economic reform in many of these countries and that private-sector promotion and commercial development would better serve these countries than traditional forms of aid. They argued that "trade, not aid" was the preferred instrument of rapid development. As a consequence, the second half of the 1990s witnessed much discussion of aid modalities and a serious attempt to bring about new dynamics on the ground and within aid agencies. Several programs were implemented specifically to promote trade possibilities for low-income countries. Aid appeared to be in crisis in the mid-1990s, with overall aid volumes recording the first sustained declines since the end of World War II.

Inevitably, the policy pendulum has now swung back to a position more favorable to foreign aid. The emergence of Jubilee 2000 and other civil-society campaigns in the West have made the public more aware of the problems of poverty and debt in developing countries. The global HIV/AIDS crisis has stimulated calls for the international community to "do something." Third World countries have lobbied the West aggressively to get more aid; in Africa, for instance, African heads of state have used the New Economic Partnership for Africa's Development (NEPAD) campaign with great effectiveness to argue that they are willing to exchange governance reforms for more aid. In the aftermath of 9/11, the role of collapsed states such as Afghanistan in harboring terrorist organiza-

---

1. A short list of key works includes Berg (1993), Boone (1996), Bräutigam (2000), Easterly (2001), Gwin and Nelson (1997), Killick (1998), Lancaster (1999), Martinussen and Engberg-Pedersen (1999), Tarp (2000), van de Walle and Johnston (1996), White (1998), and World Bank (1998).

tions has offered a new foreign policy motivation for foreign aid (Sachs 2002).

As a result, the political climate for increasing budgetary allocations for aid has improved. The Millennium Declaration adopted at the UN summit in September 2000 laid out an ambitious agenda of poverty reduction and improvements in education and health. The commitment of rich-country governments to attain the Millennium Development Goals (MDGs) that the declaration established has engendered a new dynamic of aid volume increases. Development advocates have argued that current aid volumes need to be more than doubled if the MDGs are to be reached (Stern 2003, Sachs 2002). While reaching such levels of increases appears unlikely, renewed commitment by the rich countries to increase their levels of assistance has reversed the declines of the mid-1990s. In 2002 and 2003, official development assistance (ODA) increased 11 percent in real terms, and donors have pledged to increase their aid by another 25 percent by 2006 (OECD 2004). ODA in 2003 reached $68.5 billion, the highest level ever, in both nominal and real terms (OECD 2004).

In 2001, the United Nations established the Global Fund to Fight HIV/AIDS, Tuberculosis, and Malaria in developing countries, and by mid-2003, the fund had received funding commitments of $3.4 billion from 32 countries (Summers 2003). The George W. Bush administration has led these efforts with an initial commitment of $500 million in 2001 and has promised an additional $550 million in the 2004 federal budget, in addition to the $2.4 billion set aside for its bilateral programs in the same budget.

During his run for the presidency in 2000, President Bush had seemed relatively hostile to foreign aid. His aides dismissed foreign aid as a nation-building tool that was unlikely to be successful and not particularly in the United States' national interest. In office, however, the Bush administration reacted to the new climate with promises of substantial aid increases. In addition to committing to provide substantial funding for the HIV/AIDS initiative, his administration promised in March 2002 to establish a Millennium Challenge Account (MCA) of an additional $5 billion by 2006 in support of the MDGs in the poorest countries, provided these countries adopted good governance practices and sound economic policies ("Bush, Hero or Hypocrite?" *The Economist*, May 31, 2003). The extent to which the Bush administration will come through with these funding commitments is in some doubt at the time of writing. The White House's actual budgetary proposals have been more modest than initially announced, and the administration has done little to defend its proposals on Capitol Hill. Growing budget deficit pressures also may well reduce the total new resources available for the MCA initiative ("New System Begins Rerouting U.S. Aid for Poor Countries," *New York Times*, February 22, 2004). Nonetheless, this is an impressive turnaround for an administration that came to power with the stated intention of cutting foreign aid.

This renewed commitment of rich countries to foreign aid expresses a particular concern for the poorest economies. All contend that foreign aid should be directed primarily at the several dozen least developed states, where the problems of poverty are the most severe and where, it is argued, large infusions of aid are vital to bring about economic growth. A number of observers have recently resurrected the argument about a "poverty trap" (e.g., UNCTAD 2002; Sachs 2001, 8–9). Jeffrey Sachs defines a poverty trap as a "condition, seemingly paradoxical, in which a poor country is simply too poor to achieve sustained economic growth." Different observers have advanced different theories regarding the causes of this poverty trap. In the original formulation, very poor economies could not generate enough capital surplus to reinvest in the economy. An external infusion of capital was needed to start the engine of growth. In more recent formulations, the poverty trap results from a complex of economic and institutional failures that are generated at certain low levels of economic wealth. Poverty brings about low human capital, which results in low-performing public institutions, which then undermines economic growth and maintains poverty. Many low-income economies appear to be caught in a vicious cycle in which a deficiency in one area makes success harder in others.

In an eloquent essay, Sachs (2001) argues that the existence of a poverty trap justifies a massive new infusion of foreign aid. Without the impulse of external financial and technical support, these countries are condemned to remain in poverty. Noting that aid declined substantially in the 1990s, he maintains that a massive increase in foreign aid is necessary to put the poorest countries on the path to rapid growth. The problems of the poorest countries could be overcome only if they received more aid. He points to the decline in aid levels since the mid-1990s to explain the economic records of these countries. This is debatable. In fact, declining aid in the 1990s did not prevent the best growth performance in the low-income countries since the 1970s. Indeed, the 1980s was called "the lost decade" on account of the disastrous record of economic growth, despite the fact that foreign aid was growing rapidly throughout that decade.

Proponents of large new infusions of aid dismiss as largely irrelevant the argument that large amounts of aid have not proved all that effective in the past, insisting that recent reforms in the allocation and modalities of aid will ensure that aid is more effective in the future. In 2003, Nicholas Stern, then chief economist and vice president for development economics at the World Bank, asserted that "aid is more effective today than ever before" (Stern 2003). But this too is far from clear.

This book argues that the recent reforms in aid practices, while significant, are still incomplete and partial. Their progress, moreover, has been the least in the poorest countries, where new infusions of aid are supposed to be directed. Some of the reforms constitute largely "old wine in new bottles," where a new discourse disguises how little has really changed. Other reforms are laudable but are not being fully implemented because of bureaucratic interests and political pressures within the donor community. Yet others appear mutually inconsistent, where progress in one area is likely to undermine that in another.

Large new infusions of foreign aid will largely be wasted unless the current agenda of reform is pushed forward much more aggressively. I agree with the proponents of aid and not the free-market enthusiasts who would replace aid with the magic of markets, foreign trade, and the private sector. Foreign aid has to play a critical role in any successful development strategy for these countries, but the last three decades of foreign assistance demonstrate that traditional aid programs are not effective in a number of desperately poor countries. A much more radical reform of aid remains necessary. For aid to become more effective donors must take much more careful account of the local political dynamics that undermine development in the poorest countries.

Chapter 2 identifies the several dozen most intractably unsuccessful economies in the world. It reviews the nature of governance and policy-making in these states and shows that they share political dynamics that are highly dysfunctional for economic growth. The chapter then examines the relationship between these countries and the international aid community. It argues that current aid strategies and practices have failed and need to be rethought in a radical manner. Chapter 3 discusses current aid reform proposals, and chapter 4 examines why reform of the aid system has proved so difficult. Chapter 5 offers a set of proposals for the international community to promote economic development in these countries.

2

The Stagnant Low-Income States

This chapter identifies the countries in which development has proved the most intractable during the last two decades. These countries could be said to be in a "poverty trap," if such a thing exists. I use the World Bank's list of 63 economies it identifies as low-income as the basis for creating the list of the core countries that this book is about. According to the World Bank, the poorest country in per capita income terms in 2000 was Ethiopia, with a GNP per capita of $100 (in current dollars, calculated with the World Bank's Atlas method). The richest country in the World Bank's category of low-income economies was Ukraine, with a GNP per capita of $700.

I define performance in terms of the past record of economic growth and the current level of national income. To create my list, I eliminate a total of 37 countries from the World Bank's list.

First, to focus on the poorest countries, I exclude—somewhat arbitrarily—12 countries with a GNP per capita of more than $500. This leaves 51 low-income countries. Are all of them trapped in a low-level equilibrium? In fact, many of them appear to owe their poverty to ongoing or recently ended civil conflict rather than to issues of economic governance.

So, as the second step, I exclude 12 such war-torn economies.[1] But why exclude them? It may be argued that at least some of these war-torn countries owe their current instability to their inability to promote

---

1. Afghanistan, Angola, Burundi, Democratic Republic of the Congo, Eritrea, Ethiopia, Liberia, Rwanda, Sierra Leone, Somalia, Sudan, and Tajikistan. The margin between civil war and extremely poor governance is admittedly a gray one. I do not exclude states such as Chad, for instance, judging that the civil strife that it suffered from does not qualify as a civil war.

development: Poverty led to state collapse and civil war. But in prescriptive terms, the issues of these countries are quite different from the ones I wish to address in this book, so it makes sense to exclude them. For countries mired in civil war, the best economic prescription is clearly peace rather than a new set of economic policies or more effective foreign aid. Thus, Angola is desperately poor despite its huge oil resources and despite being one of Africa's most diversified economies in the early 1970s, largely because of the persistence of civil war for over two decades. With the end of civil war in early 2003, the prospects for the country appear much better. Most, if not all, of the low-income countries undermined by civil strife and war would similarly benefit from peace, though they vary in terms of their levels of resources, human capital, and general development potential. For many of them, the end of civil strife seems predicated on the different segments of the population at war with each other coming to some basic agreement about the precise nature of the political community to which they wish to belong. If people cannot agree on the basic parameters of citizenship and nation, they surely will not be able to agree on a productive set of economic policies. In most cases, some minimal nation building has to precede state building. Past experiences with conflict management and reconstruction following the end of civil war point to a store of complex issues; the record of the international community in resolving them is clearly mixed (Ottaway 2002, Kumar 1997, Forman and Patrick 2002, Development Initiatives 2003). But these problems are distinct and need not concern us here.

Third, to focus on the countries that have been unable to sustain adequate levels of economic growth, I eliminate 12 with a growth rate of 4.5 percent or more a year during the 1990s.[2] Given a typical annual population growth rate of slightly more than 2 percent between 1980 and 2000 in low-income economies, such a cutoff eliminates all but the cases with little or no economic growth in per capita terms. Again, this cutoff point is arbitrary.

Finally, I also eliminate North Korea, both because few economic data are available for the country and because it is not a traditional recipient of aid.

The 26 economies thus identified (see table 2.1) represent the core set of countries that this book is about. Interestingly, these "stagnant low-income states" (SLIS) are more varied than one might assume. Twenty are based in sub-Saharan Africa, suggesting an African dimension to the problems of poverty, but every region of the world is represented, with one state from Central America (Nicaragua), three from Europe and Central Asia (Moldova, Kyrgyzstan, and Uzbekistan), and two from Asia (Mongolia and Pakistan). The list has relatively young states, recently

---

2. Bangladesh, Benin, Burkina Faso, Cambodia, India, Laos, Mozambique, Myanmar, Nepal, Uganda, Vietnam, and Yemen Republic.

Table 2.1   Economic characteristics of stagnant low-income states, 2000

Country	GDP per capita (PPP, current dollars)	GNI per capita (Atlas method, current dollars)	GNI (Atlas method, millions of dollars)	Total population (millions)	Average annual GDP growth, 1990–2000 (percent)	Adult female illiteracy rate (percent)	Poverty headcount[a]
Central African Republic	1,172	280	1.0	3.7	2.0	65	n.a.
Chad	871	200	1.5	7.7	2.2	66	64
Comoros	1,588	380	.2	.6	0.1	51	n.a.
Gambia, The	1,649	340	.4	1.3	3.1	71	64
Ghana	1,964	340	6.6	19.3	4.3	37	31
Guinea	1,982	450	3.3	7.4	4.3	n.a.	40
Guinea-Bissau	755	180	.2	1.2	1.2	77	49
Kenya	1,022	350	10.6	30.1	2.1	24	42
Kyrgyzstan	2,711	270	1.3	4.9	–4.1	n.a.	40
Madagascar	840	250	3.9	15.5	2.0	40	70
Malawi	615	170	1.7	10.3	3.8	53	54
Mali	797	240	2.5	10.8	3.8	66	n.a.
Mauritania	1,677	370	1.0	2.7	4.2	70	57
Moldova	2,109	400	1.4	4.3	–9.7	2	23
Mongolia	1,783	390	1.0	2.4	1.0	1	36
Nicaragua	2,366	400	2.1	5.1	3.5	33	50
Niger	746	180	1.9	108.0	2.4	92	63
Nigeria	896	260	32.7	126.9[a]	2.4	44	34
Pakistan	1,928	440	61.0	138.1	3.7	72	34
São Tomé and Príncipe	n.a.	290	.04	.1	1.8	n.a.	n.a.

(table continues next page)

Table 2.1 Economic characteristics of stagnant low-income states, 2000 *(continued)*

Country	GDP per capita (PPP, current dollars)	GNI per capita (Atlas method, current dollars)	GNI (Atlas method, millions of dollars)	Total population (millions)	Average annual GDP growth, 1990–2000 (percent)	Adult female illiteracy rate (percent)	Poverty headcount[a]
Senegal	1,510	490	4.7	9.5	3.6	72	33
Tanzania	523	270	9.0	33.7	2.9	33	51
Togo	1,442	290	1.3	4.5	2.3	58	n.a.
Uzbekistan	2,441	360	8.8	24.8	-0.5	1	n.a.
Zambia	780	300	3.0	10.1	0.5	29	86
Zimbabwe	2,635	460	5.9	12.6	2.5	15	26
Average							
All stagnant low-income states	1,415	321	6.4	19.2	1.7	47	
Excluding Nigeria and Pakistan			3.1	9.7			
Average, all low-income countries	3,963	1,230	6.3	18.7[b]	3.5	31	

n.a. = not available

a. Latest available data.
b. Excluding China and India.

Source: World Bank's *World Development Indicators 2002.*

emerged from colonial rule, as well as much older states and several states from the erstwhile Soviet Union. Other variations and distinctions among these economies will be noted later.

Of course, the number of these stagnant low-income states is somewhat arbitrary. These 26 states are not the only countries that have recorded economic growth well below their potential during the last several decades. Haiti and Armenia, for instance, are generally viewed as low-income countries with severe development problems yet just miss being in the SLIS set because of GNI per capita of $510 and $520, respectively. Cameroon and the Republic of the Congo, two very weak performers with negative per capita growth rates, have income levels just beyond my cutoff point, thanks to their significant oil resources. Had this list been conceived 10 years ago, it might have featured several different members. Similarly, in a decade, there may be additions to and subtractions from this list. Nonetheless, whatever the analytical weaknesses of my category of countries, the SLIS set will prove useful to motivate the analysis that follows, by providing an empirical face for the arguments developed.

Political Characteristics

The economic characteristics the stagnant low-income states share are well known. That they also share political characteristics is less well understood. It is worth discussing these political characteristics because they have a powerful effect on economic outcomes in these countries.

Hybrid Political Systems

The 2003 Freedom House survey of political rights and civil liberties in the world rates 9 of the 26 countries as "not free," 12 as "partly free," and 5 as "free" (Karatnycky 2004). (See table 2.2.) The "free" countries are relatively stable electoral democracies, where elections have been reasonably free and fair, and basic rights are respected. In Mali, for instance, a military regime was toppled in 1991, leading to the election of President Alpha Oumar Konaré, who was reelected in 1996 and stepped down at the end of his second term in early 2002. Amadou Toumani Touré replaced him through elections in the first peaceful electoral transfer of power in the country's history. At the other extreme, countries like Pakistan, Kyrgyzstan, and Guinea have political systems where the most basic political and civil rights are not respected, and thus they are rated as "not free."

These Freedom House distinctions are perhaps too tidy. The "third wave of democratization" in the late 1980s and early 1990s affected all these 26 regimes (Huntington 1991, Diamond 1999, Bratton and van de

Table 2.2 Political longevity in poorest countries, 1960–2003

Country	Current leader[a]	In power since	Number of leaders since 1960[b]	Average number of years in power of all leaders since 1960	FH score[c]
Zimbabwe	Mugabe	1980	1	23.0	nf
Guinea	Conté	1984	2	21.5	nf
Gambia, The	Jammeh	1994	2	21.0	pf
Malawi	Muluzi	1994	2	19.5	pf
Mongolia	Bagabandi	1997	3	14.5	f
Senegal	Wade	2000	3	14.3	f
Togo	Eyadema	1967	3	14.3	nf
Tanzania	Mkapa	1995	3	14.0	pf
Kenya	Kibaki	2003	3	13.3	pf
Kyrgyzstan	Akayev	1990	1	13.0	nf
Uzbekistan	Karimov	1990	1	13.0	nf
Zambia	Mwanawasa	2001	3	13.0	pf
Mali	Touré	2002	4	10.8	f
Guinea-Bissau	Yala	2000	3	9.7	pf
São Tomé and Príncipe	de Menezes	2001	3	9.3	f
Chad	Déby	1990	5	8.6	nf
Mauritania	Taya	1984	5	8.6	nf
Niger	Tandja	1999	5	8.6	pf
Nicaragua	Bolanos	2001	5	8.5	pf
Central African Republic	Bozizé	2003	6	7.2	nf
Madagascar	Ravalomanana	2002	6	7.2	pf
Comoros	Azali	1999	7	6.1	pf
Ghana	Kufuor	2001	9	4.7	f
Moldova	Voronin	2001	3	4.3	pf
Nigeria	Obasanjo	1999	11	3.9	pf
Pakistan	Musharraf	1999	13	3.7	nf
Average			4.3	11.4	

a. Leader in power at the end of 2003.
b. 1960 or year of independence. Leader duration averages for former Soviet states are dated from the breakup of the Soviet Union in 1990. Number of leaders does not include interregnum or temporary leaders.
c. Freedom House (FH) scores (2004): f = free; pf = partly free; nf = not free.

Sources: CIA Fact Book, author's calculations based on Bienen and van de Walle (1991).

Walle 1997). With the exception of the Gambia and Pakistan, all of them had been single-party or no-party authoritarian states two decades ago.[3] All of them underwent some political reform during the 1990s, in the context of varying degrees of international pressure, popular protests, and elite support for democracy. In the erstwhile Soviet republics, the collapse of the Soviet Union in 1991 resulted in the emergence of often unstable regimes with formally democratic institutions. In Africa, the Central African Republic, Guinea-Bissau, Madagascar, Malawi, Mali, Niger, São Tomé and Príncipe, and Zambia all underwent unprecedented democratic transitions that toppled authoritarian rulers in the early 1990s (Bratton and van de Walle 1997). As a result, 24 of these stagnant low-income states have had multiparty elections during the 1990s, in some cases for the first time in their history. These countries thus reflect the reality that at the beginning of the 21st century, the traditional single-party regime is dead, existing only in a handful of the most retrograde authoritarian states. Virtually all countries now include electoral competition and formally recognize some basic rights for their citizens. Today, all of them have governments that allow opposition parties to compete and win seats in the legislature, while an independent press is allowed to exist and nongovernmental associations are free to form and seek members. Later paragraphs will considerably nuance these achievements, but their extraordinary novelty in historical perspective must be remarked upon. Virtually no one predicted the demise of the single-party regime or the universalization of electoral politics. Indeed, the alleged superior stability and resilience of authoritarian regimes was an adage of faith of most political scientists throughout the 1970s and 1980s (Crozier, Huntington, and Watanuki 1975, Kirkpatrick 1982).

The emergence of electoral politics all over the world does not mean that liberal democracy has triumphed. On the contrary, Freedom House still ranks 49 states in the world (out of 192) as "not free" and 55 as only "partly free." In most of these cases, the presence of formal democratic institutions disguises what remains an authoritarian political system. The same holds true in many of the 26 stagnant low-income states. In Togo, for instance, a former dictator for life, President General Gnassingbe Eyadema, has been in power since a 1967 coup but adapted nicely to democratization in the early 1990s; after winning single-party elections in 1979 and 1986 with 100 percent of the valid votes cast, he won competitive contests for the presidency in 1993, 1998, and 2003, thanks to a combination of violence, intimidation, and fraud (e.g., Apedo Amah 1997).

In sum, the single-party regime has been replaced by what Larry Diamond (2002) has called "hybrid" political regimes, which combine newly

---

3. The Gambia's highly imperfect multiparty electoral regime was ended by a military coup in 1994; in Pakistan, the return to civilian multiparty rule in 1985 lasted until October 1999, when it was ended by a military takeover.

minted democratic institutions with the persistence of authoritarian practices. The regimes in all the stagnant low-income states can be characterized as hybrid, including the five "free" countries. As such, a number of other common characteristics are important to understand the governance of these states and its consequences.

"Presidentialism"

The stagnant low-income states can be characterized as *presidential* in two different but related ways. First, they are presidential in a formal sense: These states have all long had a presidential constitution, in which a president is head of state and almost invariably effectively the head of government, even when a prime minister is formally head of cabinet. They are typically strongly presidential, with a constitution that confers wide powers to the executive branch and very few to the legislature, clearly the junior partner of government. Powers that allow the legislature and judiciary to discipline the president do not exist or are limited to a difficult impeachment process requiring a supermajority, whereas the executive branch has a number of legal instruments with which to cow the other branches of government in addition to the extralegal and informal powers at the president's disposal. For instance, in most of these countries, the president has the power to dismiss the legislature and force legislative elections, one of the governmental powers usually associated with parliamentary rule. But the parliament lacks the power to impeach the president, one of the legislative perquisites associated with the balance of powers in presidential systems (Powell 2000, Haggard and McCubbins 2001; see Frye [1997] on the former Soviet republics). In sum, these regimes often combine executive advantages of both presidential and parliamentary regimes. The only effective check on presidential power is through direct elections, if and when these are free and fair.

Something of a consensus has emerged in recent years among students of Third World politics about the benefits of parliamentary government for fledgling democracies (e.g., Linz and Valenzuela 1994, Stepan and Skach 1993). Alfred Stepan and Cindy Skach's (1993) well-known finding shows that all the stable democracies among the countries that became independent after 1945 have been parliamentary and none presidential. As they conclude in an influential analysis, parliamentary government is more likely to allow for the consolidation of democratic rule because of its greater propensity for governments to have majorities to implement their programs; its greater ability to rule the constitution and its greater facility at removing a chief executive who does so; its lower susceptibility to military coup; and its greater tendency to provide long party-government careers, which add loyalty and experience to political society (Stepan and Skach 1993, 22).

Table 2.3 Developing countries with parliamentary systems

Country	GDP per capita, 2002 (PPP, current dollars)	GNI per capita, 2002 (Atlas method, current dollars)	GNI, 2002 (Atlas method, billions of current dollars)	Aid per capita, 2001 (current dollars)	Freedom House ratings,[a] 1999–2000	GDP per capita average growth rate, 1990–2001 (percent)
Bahamas	17,000	14,960	3.80	27.3	1,1,f	0.1
Bangladesh	1,700	370	48.50	7.7	3,4,pf	3.1
Barbados	14,500	9,750	2.60	−4.3	1,1,f	1.7
Belize	4,900	2,960	.75	86.6	1,1,f	1.6
Botswana	9,500	3,650	5.10	17.2	3,2,f	2.9
Dominica	5,400	3,180	.23	276.7	1,1,f	1.4
Fiji	5,500	2,160	1.80	31.8	2,3,f	1.7
Grenada	5,000	3,720	.36	114.6	1,2,f	2.9
Guyana	4,000	840	.55	132.8	2,2,f	4.4
India	2,358	450	455.00	1.0	2,3,f	4.1
Jamaica	3,900	2,820	7.40	20.9	2,2,f	−0.3
Kiribati	840	810	.77	133.9	1,1,f	0.6
Mauritius	11,000	3,850	4.70	18.1	1,2,f	3.9
Papua New Guinea	2,300	530	2.80	38.7	2,3,f	1.0
St. Lucia	5,400	3,840	.61	103.6	1,2,f	0.6
St. Vincent and the Grenadines	2,900	2,820	.33	74.6	2,1,f	2.5
Solomon Islands	1,700	570	.25	136.6	1,2,f	−1.5
South Africa	10,000	2,600	113.50	9.9	1,2,f	0.2
Trinidad and Tobago	9,500	6,490	8.60	−1.3	1,2,f	2.9

a. The three scores are, from left to right, for political rights, civil liberties, and freedom status. The first two are each measured on a one-to-seven scale, with one representing the highest degree of freedom and seven the lowest; "f," "pf," and "nf," respectively, stand for "free," "partly free," and "not free." Countries whose combined averages for political rights and for civil liberties fall between 1.0 and 2.5 are designated "free," between 3.0 and 5.5 "partly free," and between 5.5 and 7.0 "not free."

Sources: World Bank's *World Development Indicators 2003*. Data for India from World Bank's *World Development Indicators 2002*.

How successful are parliamentary regimes in the developing world? Table 2.3 lists the 19 low- and middle-income countries with parliamentary regimes and some of their characteristics. On average, they are more democratic and have enjoyed better economic performance than the presidential regimes in the developing world. Of course, many are micro island states, so it is difficult to generalize. But the presence of India and South Africa in the list suggests parliamentary rule can thrive in bigger countries as well.

Formal presidential powers in the stagnant low-income states are reinforced by a series of informal mechanisms. Executive accountability is weakened not only by the combination of constitutional provisions that insulate the presidency from the other branches of government but also by the de facto practices of power. Inadequate resources typically dilute the ability of legislatures to undertake real oversight of the executive branch. For instance, Rakner et al. (2004) report that in Malawi government funding is available only for the parliament's plenary sessions. As a result, there is no functioning committee system, though 13 committees exist on paper. These deficiencies are particularly striking in an area such as budgetary oversight. In their study of budgetary procedures in anglophone Africa, Ian Lienert and Feridoun Sarraf (2001) note several ways in which parliamentary oversight of the budget has been undermined.[4] In countries like the Gambia, Malawi, and Zambia, the budgetary auditing function was placed in the executive rather than the legislative branch. A shortage of resources has delayed and undermined reporting to parliamentary oversight committees on budgetary matters; thus in the Gambia in 2001, the last audited accounts related to the 1990–91 fiscal year (Lienert and Sarraf 2001, 14). In these and other cases, inadequate resources and short sessions have weakened the legislature, and it cannot take advantage even of its limited prerogatives to impose accountability on the executive branch (see Burnell [2001] on Zambia).

Donors and aid practices have tended to accentuate these presidential tendencies. Until very recently, the donors almost entirely ignored the nonexecutive branches of government. It was only in the 1990s that donors began to extend any technical assistance and resources to parliaments. Though judicial-sector assistance is more long-standing, at least for some bilateral donors, it remains true that the overwhelming majority of donor assistance is directed to the executive branch of government. Moreover, the donors have largely ignored the legislative and judicial branches of government in the policy dialogues conducted during the last 20 years. The emergence of parallel budget structures through which donors attempt to enforce conditionality actually weakens the ability of the legislature to provide oversight. The latest of these attempts, the World Bank's Poverty Reduction Strategy Papers (PRSPs), is analyzed in the next chapter.

A hallmark of presidentialism is the greater tendency toward weak and poorly institutionalized political parties (Mainwaring 1993). The separation of powers inherent in presidential systems weakens the legislature, where organized parties are most likely to wield power. When the presidency controls the majority party in the legislature, legislative auton-

---

4. In a review of budgetary practices in Haiti, Myers (2000) makes a remarkably similar diagnostic.

omy may in any event be pro forma. In all but three of the stagnant low-income states where party competition is meaningful, the president's party held a majority in the legislature in mid-2003; only in São Tomé and Príncipe and Mali was the president's party not the biggest single party in the legislature. Much more typically, the president's party is the dominant player in the legislature. Thus, in the Gambia in 2003, the Alliance for Patriotic Reorientation and Construction (APRC) had 50 out of 53 seats; in Mongolia, the Mongolian People's Revolutionary Party (MPRP) won 72 of 76 total seats; and in Moldova, the Communist Party of Moldova (PCM) had 71 out of 101 seats. The president uses his control over the presidential majority to weaken parliamentary power, including constitutional provisions to enforce accountability on the executive. In addition, many have rules that limit debate and make members' bills harder to bring up.

The judicial branch of government is similarly weak, both because it is starved of resources and because its independence from the other branches of government is either not recognized or extremely recent. Although most developing-country constitutions since 1945 have paid lip service to the principle of judicial independence and review (Schwartz 1999, Domingo 1999), in practice, judicial subservience to the executive branch of government has predominated. Poorly trained and underfunded judges, an often antiquated legal system, and strong legal-political pressures undermine the judicial sector's ability to function effectively, and the much more ambitious task of constituting an effective mechanism of executive accountability is almost entirely unrealistic. To be sure, judicial independence has improved in a number of low-income countries, one of the gains of the third wave of democratization (see Widner [1999] on the African cases). Yet, even in countries that have undertaken substantial recent democratization, the judicial sector continues to exhibit many traits of the previous authoritarian period, including excessive deference to the executive branch. Writing about Ghana, Kwasi Prempeh (1999) notes the continuation of a "jurisprudence of executive supremacy" since the successful return to multiparty politics and the difficulty of establishing the more desirable "jurisprudence of constitutionalism."

The SLIS regimes can be called presidential in the second sense that national politics revolves around the person of the president and his office. The president dominates a politics that is deeply personal and clientelistic rather than rule-driven or ideological (see next section). That is to say that it is impossible to understand the contemporary politics of Zimbabwe without focusing on Robert Mugabe or of Kyrgyzstan without focusing on Askar Akayev, because both dominate their political systems to an extent inconceivable in the more mature Western democracies.

One dimension of this power is longevity in office. These countries have been characterized by relatively little alternation in power, as is made clear by table 2.2. The average leader in these 26 countries has been in power 11.4 years.[5] Since 1960, they have had an average of 4.3 leaders. By way of comparison, the United States during the same period has had nine presidents, who stayed in power an average of 4.7 years, while a typical parliamentary democracy such as the Netherlands has had 12 prime ministers, who stayed in power only 3.5 years on average. The presidential stability in the stagnant low-income states is all the more remarkable given their dismal economic performance. Such longevity in office is in large part explained by the nondemocratic nature of many of these regimes, even when the countries have moved to regular nominally competitive elections in the last decade. Thus, during the last decade only one of the sitting presidents in all 26 countries lost an election. In Madagascar in 2001, Didier Ratsiraka refused to accept an inevitable electoral defeat, and his attempts to steal the election resulted in a long and costly constitutional stand-off with his rival Marc Ravalomanana, who finally was allowed to occupy the office. Otherwise, leaders in the stagnant low-income states have routinely won the elections they have competed in, sometimes with suspiciously large margins of victory.

The real significant innovation of recent democratization has been the arrival of term limits, which have forced the retirement of leaders like Daniel Arap Moi in Kenya (2003), Konaré in Mali (2002), Jean-Bertrand Aristide in Haiti (first time in 1996), or Frederick Chiluba in Zambia (2001). In these countries, the citizenry has been able to assert the legitimacy of term limits as a mechanism to circumscribe presidential power. To be sure, many leaders continue to be able to maintain themselves in power: Lansana Conté in Guinea and Eyadema in Togo managed to engineer last-minute constitutional changes to allow them third terms in 2003, despite considerable domestic and diplomatic pressures (on Togo, see *The Economist*, "Africa's Longest-Serving President: Never Togo," June 5, 2003). Nonetheless, the mantle of "president for life" that Third World dictators once wore quite officially and without reticence is no longer acceptable in all but a very few stagnant low-income states; in even highly imperfect multiparty electoral regimes, the principle that the current incumbent will one day have to step down is one of the achievements of the recent political liberalization.

The importance of alternation in power should not be underestimated. Its absence is a characteristic of many authoritarian regimes, which typically lack institutional mechanisms to effectuate a peaceful change of leadership. Even in the hybrid multiparty electoral regimes of the developing world today, the degree to which it is possible for a sitting president to lose an election provides an indication of how democratic the country really is. Recent research suggests that the absence of alternation

---

5. This average is actually somewhat lower than the true average time in power in these countries because the current leaders are all "right censored"—that is, we do not know how much longer they will be in power. See Bienen and van de Walle (1991).

in the 1990s explains the degree of democracy a country has enjoyed more than any other variable (e.g., van de Walle 2001). In other words, the longer a leader has been in power, the lower the level of political competition and participation prevailing in the political system. The longer leaders stay in power, the more power they accumulate, the more they escape accountability, and the less other political actors check their power. This lesson has long been internalized by mature democracies, which almost invariably have institutional rules, such as term limits, to limit the power of the executive. In the hybrid regimes of the developing world, where presidential dominance is little tempered by the regular multi-party elections, these term limits are even more important.

In the sense in which it is used here, presidentialism is associated with the absence of liberal democracy. The personalization of power, in which the presidency is effectively above the rules of the game and not account-able to the other political actors, is not compatible with democratic politics. To what extent, then, are the more democratic countries like Mali or Mongolia presidential? I would argue that democratization in these coun-tries involves their progressive movement away from the dynamics of presidentialism but that in the short term, these countries are likely to continue to exhibit many of these dynamics, given the weight of the past, the expectations of political actors, and the relative strengths of different national institutions.

The evolution of Mali in the 1990s demonstrates this. The emergence of the Third Republic in 1992 and the election of President Konaré was a decisive step toward liberal democracy (Smith 2001, Thiriot 1999, and Vengroff 1993). The egregious human rights abuses and patrimonial man-agement of public resources, which marked the regime of Konaré's prede-cessor Moussa Traoré (in power between 1968 and 1991), clearly ended. Most observers described President Konaré (1992–2002) as a sincere demo-crat throughout his two terms in office. Yet, presidential dominance has con-tinued to mark public life. The executive branch of government remains largely unaccountable, as attested by evidence of considerable corruption in civil service. In Mali today—unusually among the stagnant low-income states—President Touré does not command an automatic majority in the National Assembly, whose members are divided into several dozen highly volatile parties, but the constitution gives him considerable discretion over national legislation. The legislature has not emerged as an effective body for debating national policies and cannot provide real oversight of the executive branch of government. In sum, in a country like Mali, the progression away from presidentialism will be slow and arduous.

Pervasive Clientelism

Politics in the stagnant low-income states is also characterized by sys-tematic political clientelism, which can be defined as a dyadic exchange involving actors with different levels of wealth and power. Anthropologists argue that clientelism is a very important institution in peasant society, where it plays an important role of social insurance and risk management in the absence of viable state institutions (Schmidt et al. 1977). In the poorly integrated societies that emerge during the modernization process, clientelism remains pervasive because of the continuing weakness of state institutions. At every level of the political system, actors resort to the granting and receiving of favors. For poor people, clientelism is a survival mechanism, in the context of very nonresponsive public institutions, even if it rarely offers the possibility of economic redistribution. It must instead be seen as an instrument to palliate and legitimate social stratification. For politicians, various forms of clientelism help maintain support and achieve political stability. As a result, in these countries politics revolves around the giving and taking of favors. Parties are not distinguished by their policies so much as by the clientelistic networks they represent, which often take on an ethnoregional dimension.

Pervasive clientelism has several implications. Most important, even as it results from weak formal political institutions, it promotes political and sociological dynamics that further weaken those same institutions. Economic actors have low expectations regarding the ability of state organizations to meet their needs, so they go to local "patrons" for favors. As a result, shadow institutions, rather than public ones, perform key allocation processes in a nontransparent and usually highly inegalitarian fashion. Clientelism results in weak fiscal extraction, with effective privatization of a substantial proportion of government revenues. It may subvert public policy—for example, customs fraud may in effect constitute a tax on international trade, which is at odds with the government's own official trade policies.

Two somewhat distinct forms of clientelism can be identified.[6] The first form, *patronage*, can be defined as the practice of using state resources to provide jobs and services for political clientele. Robert Bates and Paul Collier (1993) estimate that President Kenneth Kaunda of Zambia personally controlled some 50,000 jobs in and around the city of Lusaka in the late 1980s. Patronage is designed to gain support for the patron who dispenses it. Almost invariably, patronage is achieved thanks to state resources, so it confers a fundamental political advantage to the incumbents, who have privileged access to these resources. In the poorest countries, patronage is limited by the fiscal constraints on the state and may thus be actually limited in comparative terms, but it is nonetheless a fundamental component of these political systems.

The second type of clientelism is *prebendalism* (Joseph 1987). This refers to the handing out of *prebends*, in which individuals are given public offices in order for them to benefit from personal access to state resources.

---

6. The following arguments are further elaborated in van de Walle (2002).

Prebends and patronage overlap but are distinct political institutions, with different economic implications. Hiring a member of one's ethnic group to a senior position in the customs office is an example of patronage. Allowing the customs officer to use the position for personal enrichment by manipulating import and export taxes is an example of a prebend.

In the language of economics, the prebendal relationship provides a classic principal-agent dynamic in which the principal has few effective means of monitoring the agent's behavior. The precise nature of the arrangement is typically ambiguous or flexible and thus unstable. In some cases, the right to benefit from state resources and appropriate public revenues is explicitly given to the officeholder. President Mobutu Sese Seko of Zaire famously commanded his ministers to enrich themselves but not "to steal too much" (Young and Turner 1985). He could not know exactly how much each of his ministers actually took in, so he regularly rotated officials in and out of office and periodically arrested a minister to scare the others. Governments know there is considerable rent seeking by officials but are unable to control its extent, even if they wished to do so (Blundo and Olivier de Sardan 2001). Alternatively, governments by necessity choose to countenance practices they know about. The state's top officials probably do not formally sanction teachers who charge an unofficial tuition to their public school students or policemen who charge cars at informal road blocks. The government often accepts such behavior because it lacks the resources to pay reasonable salaries or has accumulated arrears because of revenue shortfalls and so views such behavior as a form of informal revenue generation it cannot itself undertake.

Patronage is often perfectly legal, though it is frowned upon and constitutes a "grey area" of acceptable practice; it is present in the bureaucracies of the most advanced economies, though it is often circumscribed through various forms of codification. For example, Robin Theobald (1990, 56) cites the estimate of 4 million patronage positions in state and local government in the United States during the early 1980s. Prebendalism, on the other hand, entails practices in which important state agents unambiguously subvert the rule of law for personal gain. As a result, these practices are always illegal, even when they are endemic.

The economic cost of prebendal forms of clientelism are much greater than the costs of patronage. The latter is often, though not necessarily,[7] inefficient and tends to result in excessive government consumption. But otherwise, its negative effects on economic growth may be minimal and outweighed by its sociopolitical benefits. Certainly, a number of middle-

---

7. If the member of one's ethnic group hired at the customs office is fully qualified, honest, and hardworking, there is no cost at all. One explanation of the high growth rates found in countries, notably in Asia, in which there was clearly pervasive clientelism, is that the people who benefited from patronage performed very well.

income countries, such as Korea and Brazil, demonstrate that healthy economic growth is possible in systems with considerable levels of petty corruption and cronyism, because those governments do not systematically undermine the property rights of investors and because, despite existing flaws, the government performs many of its core functions reasonably well. In industrialized, mature democracies, such practices are even less dysfunctional because there is a large pool of qualified applicants for the offices, and minimal qualifications can be imposed even on patronage positions. Moreover, the legislature holds the executive accountable through mechanisms such as confirmation processes for higher-level appointments.

Endemic forms of prebendalism, on the other hand, imply the subversion of property rights and the rule of law and thus undermine productive forms of investment. The predatory behavior of government officials results in lower returns to private capital and thus lower rates of investment. Probably the majority of the complaints that foreign businesses make to explain their reluctance to invest in these economies concern forms of rent-seeking and corruption that are linked to prebendalism. In a study of the constraints on private-sector investment in sub-Saharan Africa, James Emery (2003) writes that "one finds an astonishing prevalence of petty obstructionist behavior by officials . . . to impose a requirement on a firm, and then act in classic rent-seeking fashion to leverage their position." He concludes that the survival of many of these practices, despite two decades of donor attempts to liberalize the investment climate, shows that they play a fundamental political function in these states. Indeed they do: Political stability is achieved at least in part by allowing enough key political elites access to the offices that will result in rent extraction.

In addition, these practices have a deeply corrosive effect on civic attitudes. In Madagascar, for instance, recent public opinion surveys reveal deep mistrust of all public officials, largely because of the perception that public officials are venal. Over 60 percent of those interviewed believed high-level corruption and the greed of political elites were the biggest obstacle to national development in the country in the mid-1990s (Razafindrakoto and Roubaud 1996). High-level corruption tends, moreover, to help legitimate petty corruption, which is more likely in these kinds of political systems.

How pervasive are these practices in the stagnant low-income states? It is hard to know exactly, but anecdotal evidence and the generally bad performance of the countries on various "rule of law" and corruption indices suggest that these practices are endemic. World Bank researchers have assembled a dataset on six governance indicators.[8] The 173 countries

---

8. See Kaufmann, Kraay, and Zoido-Lobaton (2002). The indicators are voice and accountability, political stability, government effectiveness, regulatory quality, rule of law, and control of corruption.

included were ranked for each of the six indicators, and these rankings were then averaged. The highest-ranked country—or the one with the best governance in the eyes of these researchers—is Switzerland, with an average ranking of just over 5. The highest-rated stagnant low-income state, by way of comparison, was Mongolia, with an average rank of 54. The average ranking for all of the stagnant low-income states was 114. Even allowing for anomalies in the data,[9] such numbers suggest the unusually poor governance record in these countries, even in comparison with other low-income states.

Eliminating corruption and all forms of clientelism in the stagnant low-income states is unrealistic and probably not necessary to promote economic growth and individual welfare. Some analysts point to countries like China to suggest that economic growth and relatively high levels of clientelism can coexist. Perhaps, but that does not mean that clientelism does not sometimes significantly hamper low-income economies. The discussion here has sought to show that some forms of clientelism are more damaging to the economy than others and that policymakers need to focus on eliminating or circumscribing the most damaging forms if the stagnant low-income states are to develop.

Low Capacity of Public Institutions

Another characteristic of these stagnant low-income states is the low level of capacity in public institutions, despite decades of institution building. These institutions appear incapable or unwilling to provide any of the wide number of services to their citizens. Public education and health services are of poor quality or are unavailable to substantial segments of the population, particularly outside the main urban centers. Public infrastructure is weak and poorly maintained. Government revenue collection is inefficient and undermined by considerable leakage. Governments often have a comprehensive and complex regulatory framework in place in theory, but in practice regulation of societal and economic processes is haphazard, arbitrary, and incomplete. Government officials are unable to apply some of the laws in the books but apply those not in the books.

Paradoxically, institutional capacity in many stagnant low-income states appears not to have improved over the last 30 years, despite rapid growth in the number of trained individuals available to the state and despite the sizable increase in the size and budgets of the state apparatus (Berg 1993, Bräutigam 1996; but see Goldsmith [2003] for a contrary position). To cite just one example, Zambia is said to have had fewer

9. Among other anomalies, the dataset views Zambia's regulatory environment as better than South Korea's, while Chad is viewed as the third best country in the world in terms of "corruption control," and the Gambia is suggested to have a more effective government than South Africa.

than 60 college graduates at the time of independence. Since then, the number of graduates has increased to tens of thousands, yet there is little evidence that the ability of the state to perform routine tasks has improved. On the contrary, the quality of many public services appears not to have improved or to have even declined since the mid-1970s, judging by the lack of improvement in basic welfare indicators, as well as reports about widespread public management problems (Rakner 2003). In 2001, the World Bank was arguing that "institutional weaknesses and public expenditure management" were key factors undermining the Zambian "government's ability to carry out the broad objectives of growth and poverty reduction" (World Bank 2001a, xxii).

Despite popular notions to the contrary, these countries are not easily characterized as having big bloated bureaucracies that need to be pruned (Goldsmith 1999). Examining cross-national data on the size of public employment, it is clear that the former Soviet states typically have relatively large bureaucracies, but many of the stagnant low-income states have civil services that are quite modest in size. Thus, if the former Soviet states were excluded, total civil service employment would average 1.25 percent of the total national population in the stagnant low-income states.[10] These totals are shown in figure 2.1. By way of comparison, total public employment in the OECD countries averages 7.7 percent of the total population, while that in a region of mostly middle-income countries, like Latin America, averages 3.9 percent of the population (Schiavo-Campo, de Tommaso, and Mukherjee 1997). It is true that public employment is often a disproportionate share of total formal employment in the stagnant low-income states, largely because of the weakness of the private sector. Nonetheless, in relative terms, these are small state structures, with small bureaucracies.

The most devastating effect of long-standing fiscal pressures has been the progressive erosion of civil service salaries. Unfortunately, there are few reliable time-series cross-national data on the purchasing power of civil servants in low-income countries. The stylized fact that emerges from partial and anecdotal evidence, however, is that in these countries, patronage concerns have led governments to gradually increase the *number* of public employees but often at the cost of the *quality* of the staff recruited. In part under the pressures of fiscal pressures, governments have had to manage the overall payroll, leading to a trade-off between quantity and quality. The former has prevailed, and civil service salaries have been allowed to decline over time. Again, the data are sparse but suggest sharp declines in the purchasing power of civil servants in many countries (Schiavo-Campo, de Tommaso, and Mukherjee 1997; Lienert and Modi 1997).

---

10. Data are available for just one of the former Soviet republics in the set of countries: Moldova's was 7.3 percent. With Moldova, the average rises to 1.9 percent.

Figure 2.1 Public employment in the civil service, mid-1990s
(percent of population)

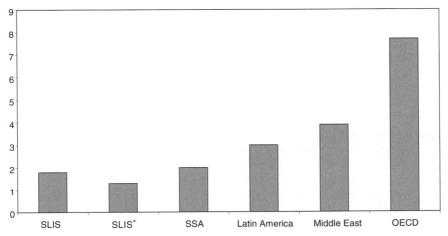

percent

OECD = Organization for Economic Cooperation and Development
SLIS = stagnant low-income states
SSA = Sub-Saharan Africa

Note: SLIS* excludes the former Soviet republics.

Source: Schiavo-Campo, de Tommaso, and Mukherjee (1997).

The choices made by the political leaders in these countries suggest that improving the capacity of public institutions is not a big priority. Civil service salaries are allowed to atrophy. It is not unusual for civil service salaries to have lost 50 to 75 percent of their real value since the 1970s (Lindauer and Nunberg 1994). Deborah Bräutigam (2000, 40) cites the example of a mid-level government economist in Kenya in the late 1990s earning $250 a month. Compare this with the monthly salaries of between $3,000 and $6,000 offered by nongovernmental organizations (NGOs) and donor projects to those same economists, which explains why the government has been unable to retain qualified staff in recent years. One should also compare the $250 with salaries in a middle-income country like Mauritius, where a permanent secretary, for example, was making $15,000 annually in 2002. Governments that value capacity and wish to build it up understand that they have to provide suitable salaries to the staff.

Similarly, the supplies and services budgets are absurdly underfunded. Civil service recruitment is politicized, and promotions are allowed to be nonmeritocratic. The independent civil service commission that existed at the time of independence has been eliminated or coopted into the control of the presidency. In fact, it makes perfect sense to believe that nondemocratic low-income country governments that rely on substantial amounts of clientelism to maintain political stability have fewer incentives to increase state capacity. Clearly, success stories such as Korea or Taiwan suggest that higher capacity does not by itself eliminate corruption. An effective system of checks and balances is probably necessary for that. Nonetheless, building the technocratic component of government, on balance, undermines the ability of political actors to engage in illicit activities.

That is not to say that there are no dedicated civil servants who sincerely wish to eliminate corruption and build more effective public management systems. Most of these bureaucracies are in fact "hybrid" administrations, which combine good and bad governance tendencies. The point is that there is always a negative synergy between state capacity and corruption. The greater the state capacity, the harder it is to engage in corruption, because of the greater likelihood of transparency and rule-based norms of behavior. On the other hand, the more corruption there is, the more a rational and effective bureaucracy will be undermined. Corrupt state agents will enhance their ability to engage in illegal activities by trying to undermine effective accounting and auditing functions, for instance. In sum, these political systems have many political actors who have an incentive to undermine the accumulation of institutional capacity. This largely explains why it has been so hard to build capacity in these countries.

Weakness of Nonstate Actors

It was argued earlier that stagnant low-income states are characterized by a low level of horizontal accountability, in which the other branches of government would be able to balance the power of the presidency. Equally important is *vertical accountability*, which refers to the extent to which state leaders are answerable to citizens—through elections, referenda, and day-to-day pressures. Perhaps the key instrument of vertical accountability is a strong civil society, but the stagnant low-income states are typically found lacking here as well, because their private sectors and civil society are weak. This weakness has important implications for political economy, because it is the powerful civic actors and interest groups that typically bring about the vertical accountability so critical to democracy and sound economic management (e.g., Przeworski, Stokes, and Manin 1999).

The structure of the economy largely explains the weakness of interest groups. The low level of industrialization and the paucity of big companies help to account for the weakness of trade unions and business associations. A small, dependent, and relatively young professional class supports an emerging but still inadequate set of professional associations that can promote and expand the civic realm. In addition, authoritarian governments long sought to prevent the emergence of independent organizations that might contest those governments' monopoly on decision making. Unions and interest groups were typically coopted and emasculated through corporatist arrangements that made them subservient to the government. Thus, many governments automatically deducted membership dues from the salaries of the public sector's unionized labor force to support an official union federation bureaucracy closely tied to the government and little interested in defending employee interests.

This situation is changing. With the onset of democratization in the early 1990s, governments are much more likely to tolerate institutional pluralism, and a wide array of interest groups, civic organizations, and special-interest associations have progressively emerged in the last decade all over the low-income world (Clark 1991, Van Rooy 1998, Hilhorst 2003, and Tripp 2003). Citizens, moreover, have turned to civic organizations to provide them with goods and services that the increasingly decrepit state no longer consistently provides. Progress is likely to be slow, as the legacy of the past and the persistence of economic difficulties will continue to undermine the emergence of the nongovernmental sector.

Perhaps the strongest and most independent single NGO in all the stagnant low-income states under review is the main trade union in Zambia, the Zambia Congress of Trade Unions (ZCTU). It was estimated to have roughly 270,000 members in the late 1990s (though fewer probably paid dues on a regular basis) (Ludwig 2001). Such a total would amount to about 7 percent of the active population in the country. Despite government attempts to control the union, it has always maintained a fair degree of independence. Indeed, the ZCTU played a key role in the political protests that ended the Second Republic of strongman Kenneth Kaunda and resulted in the election of union leader Frederick Chiluba in 1991. It has over the years consistently voiced worker concerns on economic policy and is probably the only organization in Zambia that can claim to represent more than 5,000 dues-paying members (Ludwig 2001, 162). With its relatively old mining history, Zambia's union movement is unusually strong compared with other low-income states. Union membership data are only very rarely available[11] for the 26 countries and then usually of doubtful quality. Nonetheless, it is probably fair to say that a number of these countries probably cannot claim a single organization with more than a couple thousand dues-paying members, if the central trade union federation is excluded.

---

11. The ILO's dataset on union membership does not include data from any stagnant low-income state, with the exception of Pakistan.

NGOs are weakest in the countryside, even though the majority of the population typically lives there. Again, there are significant exceptions: SYCOV, the organization of cotton farmers in Mali that emerged during that country's democratization process in the early 1990s, has proven to be a very effective representative of farmer interests and has gained very wide adhesion among the country's several hundred thousand cotton producers (Bingen 1998). But SYCOV's success is well publicized in part because it is unusual. Studies of other existing rural organizations[12] show that they are often creations of the government or highly dependent on donor funding and usually lack the autonomy that has been a hallmark of SYCOV. In this area, as in others, the current era is one of rapid change and progress, but the legacy of past neglect and sometimes repression of these groups continues to weigh heavily.

Economic Characteristics

Small Economies

The first striking similarity across the stagnant low-income states is that they are mostly very small economies. There are two striking exceptions: Nigeria and Pakistan have populations in excess of 100 million, but they are the only states in the group with a population of more than 30 million. Pakistan has enjoyed periods of sustained economic growth over the last half-century and is in my list only because of recent economic troubles. Nigeria's economic record is certainly more mediocre, but it enjoyed periods of rapid growth during its oil boom in the 1970s. If these two large country outliers were excluded, the average population of the remaining 24 economies would be 9.7 million people and their GNI $3.1 billion in 2000. Together, the 24 countries have a total population of 233 million and combined GNI of $74 billion in 2000, roughly on a par with the economy of Ireland ($86 billion) or Singapore ($99 billion), both with populations of around 4 million. Even including Nigeria and Pakistan, the combined GNI of the 26 countries was $167 billion in 2000. By way of comparison, the gross state product of Connecticut in 2001 was $153 billion and that of Massachusetts was $266 billion. In other words, and to get a sense of proportion, the modal stagnant low-income state has an economy roughly comparable in size to an average county in an eastern state of the United States.

---

12. The World Bank's Rural Producers' Organization project has tracked the most successful of these organizations in low-income countries. See the project's web page, www.worldbank.org/html/extdr/thematic.htm.

There are too many small rich countries to believe that small population size has an automatic negative effect on economic growth. The preponderance of small countries in my set of countries nonetheless suggests that these countries are hampered in some way by their "smallness." It makes sense to think that small economies have less of a margin of error, and that the market thus punishes them more than big countries for governance and policy lapses. A long-standing economics literature suggests that a smaller domestic market increases the likely efficiency losses from import-substitution industrialization (ISI) policies and trade protection, while also deterring foreign investors (e.g., Robinson 1960, Kindleberger 1984). In addition, smallness combined with certain geographic characteristics shared by these countries appears particularly disadvantageous. Eleven of the 26 states are landlocked, a situation that appears to be linked to the historically low rates of economic growth (e.g., Gallup and Sachs 1998). Twenty-four are situated in a tropical or subtropical zone. Economists have also identified this geographic characteristic as a structural disadvantage for growth. Jeffrey Sachs (2000) emphasized the prevalence of diseases such as malaria in tropical zones as a significant constraint on economic growth. Similarly, though the stagnant low-income states tend to be small, they exhibit a high degree of ethnic fractionalization, also identified in the literature as correlated with low economic growth (Easterly and Levine 1997). In fact, the SLIS are almost 50 percent more fractionalized than non-SLIS low- and lower-middle-income countries.[13]

Low Human Development

The socioeconomic characteristics of these countries are well known and need not be described in great detail. These are countries with a high level of poverty and low human capital. The World Bank estimates the average proportion of the population below the level of poverty at 47 percent. Adult literacy rates are extremely low, with an average of 71 percent for men and an abysmal 58 percent for women in 2000, putting many of these countries at below-average levels even for the category of low-income economies. The significant gender difference in literacy rates points to another characteristic of these countries: women's low status and gender discrimination. Interestingly, however, several of these countries claimed literacy rates of above 90 percent, suggesting that a simple linkage cannot be made between basic educational services and economic growth.

---

13. These findings should be treated with caution, given the large number of missing values, and conceptual and measurement problems with the ethnic data (see Fearon 2002).

Few Natural Resources

These countries are typically not well endowed in natural resources nor have fully exploited the resources they have. True, oil in Nigeria represents a significant exception. Zambia has long exploited its considerable copper reserves. Substantial oil resources were discovered both in Chad and São Tomé and Príncipe, but the oil revenues are just now coming on tap. In 17 of the 26 countries, neither oil nor minerals accounts for as much as a tenth of total exports.

Recently, economists posited a "resource curse," according to which countries with natural resources tend to enjoy slower economic growth than countries that lack them (Gelb 1988, Ross 1999, Auty 2001, Birdsall and Hamoudi 2002). The econometric studies that demonstrate this curse are noteworthy and well worth highlighting. However, before completely dismissing the benefits of natural resources, it may be useful to point out that natural resources do increase the *level* of national income, if not its *growth rate* over time. Very poor countries, such as the ones on my list, owe their poverty at least in part to the absence of natural resources, even if it is true that some resourceless countries have managed to lift themselves to higher income levels by enjoying sustained economic growth. To take just one example, it may well be true that oil-rich Gabon has not grown much faster than its neighbor the Central African Republic over the last 20 years; nonetheless, Gabon's per capita GDP is several thousand dollars higher than that of the Central African Republic, and it is comfortably a middle-income country. In part because of the corruption and venality of the Gabonese government, that oil wealth has brought much less development than one might have thought: Gabon's poverty and social indicators are only slightly better than those of the Central African Republic. But they are better.[14] The absence of significant natural resources is thus only part of the story in the poorest countries.

The Current Relationship with the World Economy

Foreign aid almost entirely mediates the stagnant low-income states' relationship with the international economy. In sum, and as shown in table 2.4, these countries receive a lot of foreign aid but relatively little foreign direct investment (FDI), and their participation in world trade is minuscule in relative terms. The importance of these countries to the global economy can be measured by their FDI and trade statistics.

---

14. For instance, life expectancy in the mid-1990s was 47 years in the Central African Republic and 52 in Gabon, while the rates of measles immunization were 37 and 50 percent, respectively. (Data taken from the World Bank's *World Development Indicators 2002*.)

Table 2.4 International economic links of stagnant low-income states

Country	Net FDI, 2000 (millions of dollars)	Total exports, 2000 (millions of dollars)	Aid per capita, 2000 (current dollars)	Total aid, 2000 (percent of GNI)	Net ODA, 2000 (millions of dollars)	Net ODA, 2001 (millions of dollars)
Central African Republic	n.a.	125.3	20	8	75	76
Chad	n.a.	233.2	17	9	131	179
Comoros	n.a.	51.8	33	9	19	28
Gambia, The	n.a.	201.8	38	12	49	51
Ghana	n.a.	2,552.9	32	12	609	652
Guinea	n.a.	777.8	21	5	153	272
Guinea-Bissau	n.a.	68.4	67	40	80	59
Kenya	n.a.	2,743.9	17	5	512	453
Kyrgyzstan	−6.9	566.9	44	18	215	188
Madagascar	n.a.	955.4	21	8	322	354
Malawi	n.a.	445.4	43	27	446	402
Mali	n.a.	574.9	33	16	360	350
Mauritania	n.a.	387.3	80	23	212	262
Moldova	127.5	640.4	29	9	123	119
Mongolia	n.a.	634.8	91	23	218	212
Nicaragua	n.a.	962.2	111	27	562	928
Niger	n.a.	282.2	19	12	211	249
Nigeria	n.a.	21,499.5	1	1	185	185
Pakistan	467.0	9,575.0	5	1	703	1,938
São Tomé and Príncipe	n.a.	15.4	236	80	35	38
Senegal	n.a.	1,335.1	44	10	424	41
Tanzania	193.5	1,324.9	31	12	1,022	1,233
Togo	n.a.	433.3	15	6	70	47
Uzbekistan	75.0	3,383.4	8	3	186	153
Zambia	n.a.	890.0	79	28	795	374
Zimbabwe	n.a.	2,245.2	14	2	178	159
Average, all stagnant low-income states	171.2	2,034.9	44.2	16	303.7	360.8

n.a. = not available; FDI = foreign direct investment; ODA = official development assistance

Source: World Bank's *World Development Indicators 2002.*

Foreign Direct Investment

Overall, the 26 countries totaled an average of udner $2 billion of the $175 billion in net annual FDI received by all the low- and middle-income countries during 1997–2000. The small amounts of FDI that accrue to these countries tend to be focused on mineral resources and oil. Thus, two substantial oil producers, Nigeria and Uzbekistan, were the only two countries that averaged a larger amount of FDI than foreign aid during 1997–2000.

Why have these countries attracted so little FDI? A complete answer is far beyond the scope of this book, but a couple of issues seem particularly salient. First, the small size of the domestic market—both because of small population and high levels of poverty and low levels of economic activity—in most of these countries makes them less attractive to foreign investment (UNCTAD 2002). Second and increasingly emphasized by scholars and policymakers who have examined this issue, these countries are not attractive to investors because of an array of governance issues. Thus, some studies have linked low investment rates to the widespread perception that political instability and corruption in these countries make them risky investments (e.g., Collier and Pattillo 2000). Others (Emery et al. 2000, Cotton and Ramachandran 2003) have emphasized the negative role still played by governmental policies and attitudes toward the private sector, which hamper not only foreign but also domestic investment. As suggested earlier, governments often subvert property rights and use regulatory mechanisms to capture rents, a practice which has a degree of political rationality but that is extremely negative for both foreign direct and domestic investment and thus tends to result in slow economic growth.

International Trade

Only six of the 26 countries had total merchandise exports in excess of $1 billion on average in the late 1990s. In seven of the countries, foreign aid actually even exceeded total exports during 1997–2000.[15] Traditional commodities dominate merchandise exports in these countries. Between 1997 and 2000, manufacturing exports constituted an average of only 24 percent of all exports, compared with 81 percent in the high-income states of the OECD, 50 percent for all low-income states, and 62 percent for all low- and middle-income developing countries. Thus, compared even with comparable states, the stagnant low-income states have not been able to generate investment in competitive manufacturing industries that would allow them to gain access to dynamic trading sectors.

---

15. The countries are Comoros, the Gambia, Guinea, Guinea-Bissau, Madagascar, São Tomé and Príncipe, and Tanzania.

Figure 2.2   ODA in stagnant low-income states, 1990–2000

billions of current dollars

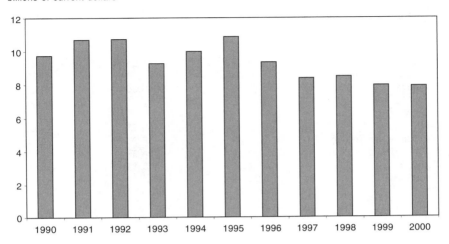

ODA = official development assistance

Source: Calculated from www.oecd.org/dataoecd.

Foreign Aid

On the other hand, these countries do receive a lot of foreign aid, as indicated by table 2.4. On average, they each received just under $340 million in official development assistance (ODA) annually between 1997 and 2000, or an average of $44 in aid per capita during the same period, amounting to 14 percent of GDP. It should be noted that this high average level disguises significant differences. São Tomé and Príncipe is one of the most aid-dependent countries in the world ($217 per capita in 1997–2000), while Moldova received a modest amount in the same years ($19.50). Several observers have lamented the sharp reduction in foreign aid during the last decade (Stern 2003, Sachs 2001). In fact, in the stagnant low-income states, the 1990s witnessed an overall decline of ODA volume of 25 percent, as is shown in figure 2.2. But this overall decline disguises very distinct evolutions, as portrayed in table 2.5. In four of the 26 countries, in Eastern Europe and Central Asia, overall aid actually increased during the 1990s. Eight countries, on the other hand, had declines of 40 percent or more during this period. All eight are sub-Saharan African cases, where declines appear linked to growing donor concerns about governance problems. The role of foreign aid in these economies is discussed in more detail later.

Table 2.5   Aid winners and losers: Evolution of ODA during the
1990s (millions of current dollars)

Country	1990–92 average	1998–2000 average	Percent change
Winners			
Uzbekistan	1.38	166.55	119.7
Kyrgyzstan	3.51	241.04	67.7
Moldova	9.70	89.79	8.3
Mongolia	68.34	214.90	2.1
Losers			
Chad	272.30	162.18	−40.4
São Tomé and Príncipe	54.14	30.25	−44.1
Central African Republic	200.25	104.37	−47.9
Comoros	52.33	25.14	−51.9
Zimbabwe	508.04	234.36	−53.9
Kenya	997.20	433.22	−56.6
Togo	227.53	89.89	−60.5
Gambia, The	103.53	40.38	−61.0

ODA = official development assistance

Source: World Bank's World Development Indicators 2002.

The Implications for Development

The preceding discussion demonstrated the striking extent to which the stagnant low-income states share certain economic and political characteristics. In particular, it seems clear that the poor economic record in these countries is linked in some way to the manner in which they are governed. What are the implications for development and, in particular, for the international community? Can foreign aid help improve this situation? The following discussion points to three general propositions.

These countries will not develop without foreign aid. The economic characteristics of these countries suggest that they require foreign assistance to spearhead the struggle against poverty. External assistance is also essential for positive change in these countries because their governments have an equivocal commitment to economic development. The governance problems described earlier prevent effective domestic policies to promote economic development. Yet a political elite in power derives benefits from the existing political status quo, and there is no reason to believe that it will be willing to give up the advantages it derives from power. Development is therefore unlikely to take place without external change agents, given the absence of a domestic political coalition that supports rapid development.

In recent years, some critics of foreign aid have argued that the West should replace aid with special incentives and policies for private-sector operators to invest in and trade with these countries. Some even argue that the current system of foreign aid prevents private-sector development and is thus directly counterproductive (e.g., Bandow and Vasquez 1994). Yet, the data presented above suggest that the rhetoric of "trade, not aid" has little to offer the stagnant low-income states, which will continue to depend heavily on the public assistance of Western donors to maintain contact with the world economy. Of course, increasing these states' share of world trade and FDI is a desirable goal, but given their governance problems and economic structure, it is unrealistic to believe that the private sector can spearhead growth by itself.

Foreign aid has to focus on creating and strengthening prodevelopment institutions. In these countries, the main objective of foreign aid should be to help bring about political and institutional change. To do so, aid has two tasks. First, it must work to increase the accountability of those in power. In all stagnant low-income states, the weakness, if not absence, of accountability of the executive branch of government has a profound development cost, and so greater accountability of the executive branch is a prerequisite for development. In a small number of countries, mostly in Asia, the absence of democracy did not prevent development. Indeed, a number of theorists have held up these "developmental dictatorships" as examples of the proposition that rapid growth and democracy were antithetical (e.g., Wade 1990). In fact, the statistical analysis of the relationship between political regime type and economic growth does not suggest an advantage for authoritarian governments (Przeworski, Limongi, and Cheibub 2000; see Leftwich [1996] and Evans [1995] for a general discussion). In any event, in the stagnant low-income states, the development failures of the last 30 years demonstrate the need to make the executive more accountable to other institutional actors.

Second, foreign aid should work to expand the capacity of state institutions to promote development. This is problematic because *clientelistic regimes have no incentive to promote state capacity for development*. Because low capacity facilitates rent-seeking and clientelistic politics, the governments in the stagnant low-income states are typically extremely ambivalent about strengthening their own capacity. In many cases, government ambivalence implies the need to privatize, deregulate, or decentralize public/state institutions in order to sidestep the executive branch, but this is only a partial solution at best because, first, rent-seeking interests within the executive branch will always have the power to manipulate these reform processes, and second, a number of pure public goods require public provision. There is no getting around the need to build state capacity. However, traditional strategies for institution building are doomed to failure. So strategies to build state capacity must be conceived that change current incentives within the state apparatus.

Some observers argue that the political obstacles to developing capacity within the state should lead the donors to promote institutional alternatives to the state. NGOs are often heralded as such an alternative. Yet, *while they are a critical complement to the central state, NGOs cannot replace it in key developmental functions.* There is no getting around the fact that the central state is the key player in low-income economies. There is a striking positive correlation between the strength of the central state and the presence of a vibrant civil society. NGOs cannot replace the state in the developmental realm for the simple reason that in practical terms, a relatively strong and effective state is probably a prerequisite for a dynamic NGO sector. Historically, at least, the rise of civil society has accompanied and interacted with the rise of strong central states. The central state is essential to the provision of basic infrastructure and key public goods like law and order, without which the NGO sector will not thrive. The same is probably true of the local government vis-à-vis the central government. These institutions can provide stopgap relief for inadequate central states, but they cannot replace them to provide long-term development.

The large volume of aid to these countries in the past has not achieved the desired goals. Most of the stagnant low-income states are highly aid-dependent, based on even a loose definition of this concept. Given the importance of aid to countries whose marginal economies have few links to the global economy, foreign aid should play a fundamental role in their economic growth process for the foreseeable future. It may be argued that these countries do not get too much aid. But it is difficult to believe the argument—at least in the absence of a major rethinking of the relationship between donors and recipient governments—that a massive infusion of yet more aid will bring about a structural transformation of these economies. These issues are further explored in the next chapter.

3

The Contradictions of Current Aid Doctrines

Foreign aid has benefited many Third World economies. Improvements in education levels and life expectancy, declines in poverty levels and infant mortality rates, and growth in economic production can all be linked at least in part to the actions of foreign aid donors (World Bank 2002a). Nonetheless, by the end of the 1990s, the donor community itself agreed that aid had been least effective in the poorest countries, where a substantial flow of resources had been least successful in generating the desired improvements in national welfare levels. The poor economic performance of the stagnant low-income states (SLIS) reviewed in the last chapter suggests that international efforts have been particularly frustrated in these economies.

What should the donors do to promote economic development in the stagnant low-income states? A remarkable consensus had emerged by the late 1990s among observers of the aid business about what was wrong with the traditional relationship between donors and low-income aid recipients as it had evolved since the end of World War II. First, there appeared to be general agreement that traditional aid conditionality had failed. Far from constraining governments or forcing them to adopt new policies, a large volume of aid to the low-income countries actually often served to sustain the nondevelopmental governments in power, which might have fallen without this external support. Second, the aid community agreed that the ineffectiveness of aid was often due to its failure to elicit "local ownership." Foreign aid engaged in a number of practices that ignored or exacerbated problems of local ownership and capacity building, thus often actually weakening the public institutions that might have promoted development (e.g., Bräutigam 2000, Knack 2000).

Foremost has been the problem of donor fragmentation: too many unco-ordinated projects by too many donors. Third, state-led development strategies were generally viewed to have failed. Though the donors rarely acknowledged their own role in this failure, they argued that low-income states typically took on too many tasks and did not concentrate on the core economic functions of the state, despite their very limited resources and capacity. The general consensus among the donor community came to be that states should focus on a small set of activities and allow private actors to take on more tasks.

In sum, many observers agreed that *aid was simultaneously propping up states and keeping them weak and incapable of spearheading development.* Donors were directing a massive amount of resources to corrupt and incapable states without exacting anything in exchange. Too many low-income countries were suffering from "aid dependence," in which a large volume of aid and various donor practices were combining to undermine local ownership of the development process and the generation of institutional capacity.

This chapter examines the donor community's response to the three general lessons in the stagnant low-income states. The main theme I develop is that too little real change has taken place. Aid continues to provide low-income country governments with the wrong incentives. Too often, aid resources continue to actually help sustain governance deficiencies that have a directly negative effect on development. To be sure, donor solutions to past aid failures have resulted in some successes, but the solutions are often inappropriate for the poorest low-income countries, for which other solutions need to be devised. In addition, the solutions donors prefer are often the most convenient ones for their organizations and do not necessarily have much traction on the ground. Other, less comfortable lessons have been sidestepped and ignored, yet they are probably just as essential for truly effective foreign aid in the 21st century and for the economic renewal of the stagnant low-income states.

From Conditionality to Selectivity

Donors have always sought to impose conditions in exchange for their aid to recipient governments. But the number and stringency of the conditions grew rapidly in the 1980s, when donors came to believe that government policies and management practices were the primary cause of aid's failure to promote economic development. The emergence of structural adjustment lending in the 1980s generalized the practice of policy conditionality, in which loans were extended in exchange for macro and sectoral policy reforms on the part of the government. The mediocre performance of the first two generations of structural adjustment lending resulted in a deepening of conditionality, even as most evaluations of structural adjustment criticized the donors' intrusive micromanagement that conditionality entailed. By the mid-1990s, conditionality had moved beyond narrow economic policy to focus on a wide array of sectoral and governance issues.

Conditionality proved ineffectual. To be sure, in many cases governments undertook the measures they had agreed to, which they would not have undertaken without external pressures. In addition, in particular instances, specific donors played hardball with a recipient government and cut aid sharply in response to governmental failure to implement agreed-to conditions. More generally, however, a number of studies (Killick 1998; Collier 1997; Mosley, Harrian, and Toye 1995) suggest that governments often did not implement conditions to which they had agreed, reversed reforms they had implemented as soon as donor support ended, or implemented agreed-to conditions but simultaneously introduced new policies that caused the same negative effects. Too often, governments agreed to implement policy changes with which they did not agree or for which they lacked some combination of the necessary commitment and capacity. On the other hand, governments also probably undertook some conditions—and received money for them—that they would have implemented even without donor pressure.

Some donor practices limited the effectiveness of the donors' own conditionality. For instance, every study of structural adjustment has argued that donors tend to impose too many conditions (e.g., Mosley, Harrian, and Toye 1995; Killick 1998). Conditional loans became "Christmas tree" operations in which donor personnel were tempted to add their own pet conditions, with little strategic thinking about priorities or implementation difficulties. Numerous internal World Bank reviews of its structural adjustment lending recommended limiting the number of conditions (World Bank 1986, 2001b). Yet the number of legally binding conditions in adjustment loans signed in fiscal 1999–2000 were still twice as high as those signed during 1980–84 (World Bank 2001b, 80, figure 42), suggesting how difficult it has been for staff in donor agencies to undertake necessary changes, a theme to which I return in the last chapter.

Donors, moreover, found it difficult to penalize governments that did not comply with conditionality, either because they did not fully understand the low level of compliance or because pressures to lend outweighed concerns about noncompliance. As Elliott Berg (2000, 300) has argued, "none of the parties to a structural adjustment program want it to fail. A cessation of disbursements is a personal defeat for responsible donor staff and the organizations they work for." Perversely, evidence suggests that governments that did not comply with donor conditions did not receive less external support (Burnside and Dollar 2000). In fact, one study (Alesina and Weder 2002) suggested that there was a positive correlation between corruption and aid during the 1980s and 1990s—more corrupt countries actually got more aid on average than less corrupt ones. In effect, governments faced disincentives to comply with the donors to change their policies or improve their governance. The toothless nature of conditionality has been blamed for the ineffectiveness of much aid, particularly to low-income countries undergoing economic policy reform.

The new critiques of conditionality have focused on the fact that it was applied in an ex ante manner—in other words, aid was provided before governments had actually undertaken the measures to which they had agreed (Collier 1997). By the late 1990s, donors were moving to ex post conditionality strategies in which aid would reward governments only after they had undertaken reforms agreed to with the donors or even after the reforms agreed to had started to generate the appropriate outcomes. In other words, from providing funding to encourage a government to change its health-sector policy, donors like the World Bank have sought to move to the practice of waiting for the government to change its policy for that sector, or for the rate of immunization to go up, before providing foreign aid. In this logic, donors "select" recipients on the basis of their performance (Collier 1997, White and Dijkstra 2003). What has come to be called the "selectivity" approach has the advantage of establishing much more rational incentives for low-income country governments, since aid will now focus on those that are actually undertaking what the donors believe to be growth-friendly economic policies. As William Easterly (2003, 13) has shown, the need for greater selectivity has featured periodically in donor rhetoric since at least the presidency of John Kennedy. Nonetheless today, the donor community has reaffirmed its intention to replace conditionality with selectivity.

The main implication of a selectivity-driven aid program is that countries that cannot improve their policies and governance receive a sharply reduced volume of assistance. Proponents of selectivity approaches rarely admit to this politically incorrect prospect and instead state rather vaguely that aid to these countries could easily be redirected to the NGO sector until the governments improve their performance. Thus, an OECD report on what the organization has euphemistically called its "difficult partnerships" warns that pulling out of countries has the "potential of worsening the situation" and calls instead for a "pragmatic selection of those governmental and non-governmental agencies that share a commitment to poverty reduction" (OECD 2002, 3). Since these countries typically have few such governmental agencies and a weak and underdeveloped NGO sector with limited absorptive capacity, as was discussed earlier, the inevitable implication would be a sharp reduction of aid. In recent years, moreover, when donors have responded to governance deficiencies by reducing aid to the government, the total amount that has been redirected to the nongovernmental sector has in fact been quite small—perhaps because of downward pressure on aid volume. In practice, a reduction of aid to the government has meant a similar reduction in overall aid.

To what extent have the donors increased their selectivity in the last decade? While still early to judge, studies suggest at best a mild increase in overall selectivity in the late 1990s and early 2000s. The World Bank (2002a) itself argues that its lending has undergone such a shift toward greater selectivity that in the late 1990s what it defined as "good policy" countries received almost twice as much aid as "bad policy" countries. However, Easterly (2003, 13) examines the Bank's claims and finds they are based on several key assumptions and restrictions. For his part, Easterly (2001) finds no evidence of greater selectivity in Bank lending relative to either economic policies or general governance criteria. In his 2001 book, he echoes earlier research by Alberto Alesina and David Dollar (2000). Nancy Birdsall, Stijn Claessens, and Ishac Diwan (2001) find evidence of growing selectivity in multilateral lending, with respect to economic policies, in countries with lower overall debt levels. David Simon (2002) finds tentative statistical evidence for selective lending within Africa, based on governance criteria. For his part, Eric Neumayer (2002) finds little correlation between the quality of governance and the allocation of debt relief.

All this conflicting evidence suggests that any move toward greater selectivity is partial and inconsistent. Certainly, some of the most egregious performers of the past now receive a sharply reduced volume of foreign aid. It now seems incredible that the Mobutu Sese Seko regime in Zaire was at one point one of the leading recipients of aid or that Gnassingbe Eyadema's regime in Togo received $3.1 billion in official development assistance (ODA) between 1980 and 1997. In 2000, Togo received only $70 million, roughly a third of the levels it had received in the early 1990s, suggesting that President Eyadema's heavy-handed political techniques and the high levels of corruption in Togo had finally exhausted the donors' patience. A testimony to that patience, on the other hand, is the fact that Togo had continued to receive substantial external funding into the late 1990s, amounting to over $140 million a year, or 12 percent of GDP, as recently as 1996–97. Moreover, former Soviet republics like Uzbekistan and Kyrgyzstan, which benefited from sharp rises in aid during the 1990s, were neither democratic nor particularly committed to promarket policies, while fledgling democracies in Mali and São Tomé and Príncipe were not spared the same declines in foreign support as most of their authoritarian neighbors.

A closer examination of the evolution of ODA reveals contradictions in the application of selectivity that are remarkably similar to the previous problems with the application of conditionality. First, selectivity is applied inconsistently. In some countries, donors appear to care more about governance issues, while in others they focus on the quality of macropolicy. Donors are very strict with one regime and complacent about the problems in another. One problem is that the move to selectivity does not eliminate complex issues relating to how donors should assess performance and what the precise parameters with which to evaluate success and failure should be (Adam and Gunning 2002). How much should donors weigh progress in policy performance as opposed to overall level? How quickly should donors punish policy lapses? These are very difficult questions to which reasonable people will provide different answers.

Another more serious problem is that all donors do not have the same preferences. One difficulty is of course that the link between policies and economic performance is not as strong as what the early proponents of the selectivity approach assumed. Several studies have cast doubt on the argument that there is an easily identifiable set of economic policies that helps make aid more effective and economic growth more likely (Tarp 2000; Easterly, Levine, and Roodman 2003). In part as a result, and despite the appearance of a growing consensus on policy matters under the general rubric of "the Washington Consensus,"[1] all donors are not selective in the same manner. At the most general level, the international financial institutions (IFIs) have sought to focus aid on countries based on the quality of their macroeconomic policies and have paid much less attention to issues of political governance, regarding which the IFIs have traditionally been uncomfortable. On the other hand, some bilateral donors have attached less importance to economic policy lapses but have paid much greater attention to governance issues and political performance.

Even if every donor is perfectly consistent in the application of a selectivity strategy—which is far from the case—it can still be true that overall aid allocation is not selective in any single dimension. In other words, to work, selectivity requires *donor coordination*, which has not improved significantly over the last two decades.

Second, and perhaps even more serious for the stagnant low-income states, selectivity strategies undermine needs-based strategies. As a common joke within the aid community goes, a rigorously applied selective strategy will result in aid being extended only to the Netherlands or Switzerland, given their unequaled record on governance and macropolicy. In fact, the model country for the selectivity-based allocation of aid is the "poor but virtuous" country, where the presence of extensive poverty combines with a well-intentioned and legitimate government. Unfortunately, there are few such countries. As I argued earlier, the overwhelming majority of the stagnant low-income states combine poor economic performance with governance problems and corruption. Indeed, their poverty results in large part from their lack of virtue. The exceptions are

---

1. The "Washington Consensus" (a term coined in 1989) refers to a set of economic policies, including fiscal discipline, price liberalization, trade reform, deregulation, and privatization, around which, allegedly, a broad consensus formed among economists at the leading Washington institutions focusing on development (Williamson 1993).

often new regimes: New, democratic governments emerged in the mid-1990s in two (Mali and São Tomé and Príncipe) of the five stagnant low-income states judged to be "free" by Freedom House in 2003. Because such governments should clearly not be held responsible for the disastrous performance of their authoritarian predecessors, they are an obvious target for increased aid in the context of selectivity strategies. How have they fared? In fact, both countries were rewarded with a minor "democracy dividend"; in real terms, their aid declined slightly between 1990 and 2000, albeit not to the same extent as some of their authoritarian neighbors.

Paradoxically, the emergence of the doctrine of selectivity in the donor community has come at the same time as a renewed call for attention to poverty alleviation and need-based priorities. Donors like the British Department for International Development (DFID) or the World Bank under James Wolfensohn, for instance, have moved toward explicitly focusing on social services and poverty reduction—at the same time as they have argued for rewarding good "policy performance." To be sure, the promise to focus aid on the neediest has often been made in the past but usually has been observed indifferently. Need-based aid is superficially attractive in political terms, as it allows governments to play up the humanitarian dimension of aid and defuse the populist criticism that aid is in effect "taxing poor people in rich countries on behalf of rich people in poor countries." But foreign policy and commercial motivations invariably carry larger political constituencies in donor countries than do humanitarian motivations for foreign aid, not a negligible advantage in periods of tight national budgets. That is why various studies suggest that the proportion of overall aid going to the neediest has not substantially increased during the last several decades.[2]

Some analysts within the World Bank appear to view selectivity and poverty alleviation strategies as compatible when they argue that the adoption of appropriate economic policies is a prerequisite of economic growth and poverty alleviation (e.g., Collier and Dollar 2000). In practice, however, it is difficult to believe that a rigorously applied selectivity strategy would target countries with the greatest need for poverty alleviation, and it is disconcerting that donor rhetoric often downplays the contradiction in promoting need-based and selectivity approaches at the same time.[3] Donors have the choice between not assisting the poorest countries because of their policy deficiencies and governance problems and being inconsistent in their application of the selectivity strategy. In fact, donors have typically chosen the latter approach.

---

2. For instance, see the severe judgment of Howard White (1996). For a somewhat different perspective, see Collier and Dollar (2000).

3. See Boyce (2002) for a similar argument.

Consistency being the hobgoblin of small minds, this is not necessarily a bad thing. The flexible application of selectivity principles, in which donors combine a concern for good economic policies and governance practices with poverty alleviation, without being tied to any preset standards, could lead to reasonable outcomes. Donors could judiciously balance the two imperatives. They could impose stricter policy and governance requirements in middle-income countries, in which poverty concerns are less pressing, while relaxing selectivity criteria in the poorest countries. In some borderline countries, the judicious provision of foreign aid might leverage important improvements in policies and governance. In other cases, a positive trend in policy and governance might be a better justification for donor assistance than overall level. Improving situations might justify external support even if they fell short of a predefined minimal threshold. Donors have to make judgments about the impact of their support on the evolving situation in the recipient country.

Nonetheless, why would donor organizations be able to make these judgments more wisely today than they did in the past? Some advocates of a sharp increase in foreign aid suggest that the motivations for foreign aid have dramatically changed in the recent past, so that aid allocation is more likely to be rational today. In particular, the end of the Cold War stopped donors like the United States from providing support to strategic allies like Mobutu in Zaire. Such justifications exaggerate recent historical discontinuities. Other, equally pressing foreign policy concerns are likely to shape US foreign policy, as the current debates concerning the role of aid in the struggle against world terrorism demonstrate. Indeed, the United States has been rapidly increasing its aid to Central Asian dictatorships. It provided $70 million in economic assistance to Uzbekistan in 2002, though the US Agency for International Development (USAID) itself recognized that the country's leadership "remains entrenched in a closed and stagnant political and economic system" (USAID 2003). It would be naive to believe that such foreign-policy pressures will not continue to shape foreign aid allocation decisions.

In addition, a quick examination of the record suggests that Cold War concerns shaped US aid allocation patterns much more than was the case for any other donor. For the other bilateral donors, ideological and commercial considerations were far more important in the allocation and implementation of aid programs during the 1970s and 1980s (Lancaster 2000). Thus, France's large aid program in Africa has been motivated by commercial and historical links with its former colonies, with Cold War considerations being of second-order importance (Cummings 2000, Chipman 1989). Much the same could be said for Japan. Such considerations will remain pertinent for the foreseeable future for most donors.

Debates within the Western donor community over which developing countries should receive debt relief provide a good example of how hard it is for donors to stick to strict developmental criteria in the determination of the recipients of aid resources. The evolution of the criteria that the heavily indebted poor countries (HIPC) debt initiative has used since 1996–97 provides an illustrative case study (Birdsall, Claessens, and Diwan 2001; Neumayer 2002). The initially very strict criteria required governments to demonstrate a clear and unambiguous commitment to economic policy reform over several years, such that only a small number of countries would have been eligible for debt relief. This list of criteria was then considerably expanded as a result of pressures on the donors from various sources. Key academic analysts argued for broader coverage and more generous terms, while the NGO community sought more flexible conditions and a larger net flow of resources to the indebted countries, and individual donor governments pleaded for a relaxing of conditions on behalf of specific developing countries. For some countries, it was humanitarian pressures that resulted in greater inclusion; in others, a former colonial power pleaded the case, while in yet others, defensive lending pressures within the IFIs were at work (e.g., Sachs et al. 1999, Kapur 1997).

The final list of HIPC recipients turned out to be much broader and less selective. Indeed, Cameroon became one of the first recipients of debt relief in 1999, despite having won the dubious distinction of being chosen as the most corrupt country in the world by Transparency International the previous year (van de Walle 2001, 188–89). Still, the argument that the HIPC initiative has not generated enough volume of debt relief has continued to dominate criticism of the initiative, and the ability of governments to meet the original criteria has all but been forgotten. In a characteristic analysis, the British daily *The Guardian* ("Hypocrisy that Underlines HIPC," January 29, 2003) recently blamed only the donors for the amount of relief that was reaching debtor states and did not make a single reference to the ability of governments to meet the selection criteria: "The basic problem with the Cologne deal," the newspaper contended, "as with every previous attempt to reduce Africa's debt burden, is that the West's criteria for sustainability do not have anything to do with human needs, but were based on narrow financial parameters."

The Washington debates about the Millennium Challenge Account (MCA) during 2002–03 provide another case study of these dynamics (Radelet 2003, Brainard 2003). The criteria for eligibility discussed initially were strict enough that fewer than a dozen states qualified for this new bilateral aid program. Clearly, such a small list of countries would not be able to justify the full $5 billion program amount that President Bush initially proposed. Either the program would be redefined or its budgetary envelope would have to be substantially reduced, clearly highlighting the tension between aid volume and selectivity. Within nine months of President Bush's initial presentation of the account at the Monterrey Summit in March 2002, discussions within the administration included

the possibility of expanding the program to lower-middle-income economies, including China and Egypt. Though they are strategically and com-
mercially important to the United States, neither has a particularly good
governance record, and US foreign aid to Egypt has long been viewed
as mired in inefficiency. By 2004, the administration was backing away
from establishing explicit criteria for eligibility and moving toward a less
transparent selection mechanism. In fairness, officials were still arguing
for a program that would be driven by strict performance standards, but
the jury was still out regarding how such a program would in the end
be implemented. Also by 2004, the MCA's original envelope of some $5
billion had been sharply reduced; the fiscal 2004 administration request
made public in late 2002 totaled just $1.3 billion (Brainard 2003). The
administration argued this was justified by the need to scale up over
time and did not affect its support for the initial scope of the program,
but many observers in Washington viewed the proposal as extremely
vulnerable to growing budgetary pressures, with the 2005 federal budget deficit estimated at more than $500 billion.

Diplomatic donor pressures from aid recipients are likely to further
dilute the donors' ability to enforce selectivity policies. Thus, for instance,
a number of African governments have signed on to the New Economic
Partnership for Africa's Development (NEPAD) initiative, in which they
promise to undertake a number of governance and policy reforms in
exchange for a larger volume of aid. Despite considerable skepticism by
much of the academic community (e.g., Chabal 2002), NEPAD has been
offered up by the donor community as evidence that African governments
have accepted the need for the kinds of policy and governance reforms
they have long advocated.[4] A large majority of African states have signed
on to NEPAD, including long-standing authoritarian leaders who never
showed much inclination for reform. President Thabo Mbeki of democratic South Africa has been the public face of NEPAD. But five of the 15
governments represented in its implementation committee are regimes
rated by Freedom House as "not free" and another 3 as "partly free."[5] Yet,
by officially committing African states to the donors' agenda of reform,
NEPAD pressures donors to lessen aid selectivity and push aid volumes.

Donor Fragmentation and the Search for Ownership

A second general critique of development practices linked the absence
of donor coordination, donor micromanagement of aid, and the lack of
local ownership. Poor aid coordination and the resulting donor frag-

---

4. Thus some World Bank officials have publicly expressed enthusiasm for NEPAD. See
Madavo (2002). To be sure, very little donor money has actually gone to support NEPAD.

5. The "not free" states are Algeria, Cameroon, Egypt, Rwanda, and Tunisia.

mentation have long been viewed as counterproductive. The lack of aid coordination imposes two big obstacles to aid effectiveness. First, the absence of coordination has a negative effect on government management of aid. In some cases, the government is truly dedicated to development and actually wants to rationalize the aid, monitor it, and better integrate it into its overall development strategy. For such governments, scarce managerial resources are wasted grappling with the plethora of donor projects and programs. On the other hand, when the government is not all that dedicated to development, the absence of coordination provides an additional excuse for the government not to exercise any ownership over the aid it receives. The technocratic element in such governments, which would like to rationalize public management, is frustrated and disempowered in relation to the rent-seeking officials, for whom the confusion and complexity of the aid system provide a useful cover in which to engage in nondevelopmental activities. Clearly, uncoordinated aid is one of the primary causes of low ownership in low-income aid recipients.

Second, the absence of donor coordination militates against the implementation of other major donor objectives. One donor's independent allocation decisions can undo the positive effects of other donor decisions. For example, one donor's conditionality will be largely pointless if other donors do not collaborate and reinforce the signals being sent to governments and markets. This was true during most of the 1970s and early 1980s, for instance, when Scandinavian support helped undermine IFI conditionality in east and southern Africa. This was one case in which bilateral support was explicitly designed to lessen the sting of another donor's conditionality. Another such example was French support for authoritarian regimes in Cameroon, Togo, and Burkina Faso in the early 1990s, which sought to help these countries compensate for IFI conditionality on the economic front, on the one hand, and bilateral conditionality on the governance front, on the other (van de Walle 1993, Banégas and Quantin 1996, Médard 1999). One result was that overall aid levels did not decline for the francophone states, except in the case of Togo, even though certain bilateral programs (such as US aid) were cut substantially.

Despite these well-known problems, donor coordination has made remarkably little progress in recent years. In their study, Arnab Acharya, Ana Fuzzo de Lima, and Mick Moore (2003) find that the number of bilateral aid donors and projects in developing countries continued to increase faster than the amount of aid actually disbursed during the 1990s (see also Knack and Rahman 2004). The primary bilateral donors were present in an average of 107 countries in 1999–2001. Table 3.1 provides the view from the recipient side. Acharya, Fuzzo de Lima, and Moore (2003) estimate that the median recipient government interacted with 23 official donors in 1999–2001. Since the last decade has seen the rapid growth of NGOs and other "unofficial" donors, it is almost certainly true

Table 3.1 Distribution of aid recipients by the number of donors, 1999–2001

Number of recipients	Bilateral donors only	Bilateral and multilateral donors
With 1 to 9 donors	34	13
With 10 to 19 donors	93	27
With 20 to 29 donors	22	69
With 30 or more donors	0	40
Average number of donors	14	26
Median number of donors	16	23

Source: Acharya, Fuzzo de Lima, and Moore (2003).

that the managerial burden of aid on recipient governments has increased in recent years. For instance, the authors note that in Vietnam 25 bilateral donors, 19 multilateral donors, and 350 international NGOs were implementing over 8,000 distinct aid activities in 2002 (Acharya, Fuzzo de Lima, and Moore 2003, 3).

By almost any criteria, most low-income countries have too many donors and projects. Given the donor predilection for a physical presence in the country and a well-balanced portfolio of project activities and resident experts, the large number of projects almost certainly imposes efficiency costs—in unrealized economies of scale and scope. In addition, it imposes significant transaction costs. The minister of health has to meet with all the donors who choose to provide assistance to the health sector; someone has to read and sign off on each of the project identification papers, project proposals, quarterly project reports, evaluation mission reports, annual reports, technical project reports, and final evaluation reports. This represents a significant burden for qualified local officials. In addition, the pressure to hire good local professionals, and the ability to pay wages well above the levels of the civil service, means that donors and international NGOs are constantly drawing away off the most effective and entrepreneurial civil servants, thereby robbing governments of capacity—a problem noted repeatedly in documents on the aid environment.

A 1999 OECD report on foreign aid in Mali linked donor fragmentation to problems of local ownership. It found that as many as a third of all official donor projects had established parallel management structures and were not completely integrated into national ministerial agencies.[6] Donor projects benefited from import tax exemptions, which, the report argued, generated an unhealthy parallel procurement process. The con-

---

6. Mali is not unique in this regard. A recent World Bank report argued that independent project implementation units were "pervasive" in low-income countries (World Bank 2003a, 33).

siderably higher salaries paid by projects also created substantial distortions in local labor markets. The report concluded that the central government did not coordinate the aid, adding that "sectoral ministries submit and negotiate project proposals directly with the donors, when it is not the latter themselves who generate the proposals they wish to receive" (OECD 1999, 7, own translation of French document).

The report noted several other costs to the absence of coordination. One particularly striking weakness is the poverty of information about the overall system of aid. The report noted, for instance, that it was impossible to determine the number of foreign experts in a country at any given time or the total number of consultant visits in the previous year (p. 24). Similarly, it was impossible to determine the government's own contribution to the projects it had agreed to or, presumably, the future obligations it had incurred to ensure the sustainability of the projects.

Virtually all recent reform proposals argue that aid should better promote local *ownership* of the development process. Ownership is in this case a euphemism for two somewhat distinct objectives: First, some observers emphasize government ownership—the engagement and commitment of government officials in the design, implementation, and evaluation of aid activities. One of the policy recommendations of the aid effectiveness studies of the 1990s was that foreign aid should be better integrated into the central state's national development management structures (World Bank 1998, van de Walle and Johnston 1996). Current calls for greater government ownership reflect a prevailing view in the donor community that the passivity and low involvement of recipient governments in aid programs lessen their impact and sustainability (World Bank 1998). Governments that are more involved, goes the argument, will go the extra mile to ensure program success.

Second, for others—particularly those in the NGO community—ownership has come to mean something rather different: They advocate the need for more active participation of local populations and stakeholders in decision making. The argument here is that local populations and NGOs can improve the performance of both donors and the government in the implementation of aid projects. Rather than empower recipient governments, this view promotes the role of nongovernmental actors in the aid process. There is a long history of evidence that the involvement of stakeholders in aid projects improves their design and implementation (e.g., Chambers 1983; Isham, Narayan, and Pritchett 1995). There is also some evidence that participatory processes make the government somewhat more responsive and accountable and thus improve its performance over time.

Little evidence is available, however, that enhanced participation will help align government policy and donor objectives in the country, suggesting that these two distinct definitions of ownership are not necessarily complementary. It is far from clear that government officials are more likely to feel committed to programs and policies that donors are pressing them to adopt because external agents have empowered a coalition of local actors to participate in decision-making processes. On the other hand, governments that are committed to a course of action they have negotiated with the donors are unlikely to look with favor on participatory processes that slow down or undermine policy implementation. The current donor rhetoric on ownership tends to obscure the tensions in these two versions of ownership, preferring a feel-good and rather vague view of local politics.

There is little doubt that the level of government ownership of donor-supported development activities can be quite low. For a variety of reasons, government officials agree to implement aid projects that they do not support. First, in some cases, the lack of technical capacity within the government accounts for the inability of the government to communicate its preferences to the donors. The latter may not have been receptive to the expression of those preferences, in any event, if they conflict with donor objectives. The pressure to move money and maintain program schedules can make the donor organization prefer its own proposals, often generic "off-the-shelf" projects that are easier to implement quickly. Second, governments may disapprove of the project objectives but desire some of the benefits of the donor support—from the finance the donor will provide for the procurement of vehicles, computers, and office equipment to the placement of nationals in overseas training programs (Berg 1997, 2000).

Ownership is particularly problematic in the stagnant low-income states, with their characteristic combination of low capacity, uncertain commitment to economic development, and various governance deficiencies. There are no hard systematic data on levels of government ownership in these countries, but in a majority of the projects that fail, evaluations note the telltale signs of an absence of government support: counterpart support from the government was never delivered as promised; key positions went unfilled for long periods of time; relevant ministries did not collaborate with the project; governments distanced themselves publicly from the objectives of the project, which in some cases contradicted stated government priorities; and, most telling of all, project outputs were not sustained following the end of donor support. Of course, low ownership may simply reflect the fact that an aid activity has failed. Governments are far more likely to actively support popular projects that are clearly successful and less likely to support ill-conceived projects that are failing. Nonetheless, insofar as local knowledge and complementary government activities can improve the design of a project and its likelihood of success, the active collaboration of the government throughout the life of a project is clearly desirable.

To promote ownership, the literature argues that donors should involve governments in the early phases of the aid cycle: Local officials' preferences should weigh more in decision making. Donors should not anticipate government needs but wait for governments to make explicit requests for assistance. In addition, it is proposed that aid activities be better integrated into the government's own development activities. In the past, aid projects were too often consciously put on a parallel track—outside of ministerial structures—with their own separate budgets, non-civil service staff, and distinct procedures. The striking proliferation of these independent project units in the 1980s and the near total absence of donor coordination proved to be a tremendous managerial burden on governments, which could not monitor literally hundreds of aid projects and therefore came to view them as the exclusive responsibility of the donors. To promote ownership, donors are being urged to decrease the number of independent projects and integrate aid into the government's own programs (van de Walle and Johnston 1996, World Bank 2000).

The PRSP as a Solution?

Donors have long sought to promote aid programs that were better integrated into government development activities. Since the late 1980s, several bilateral donors have experimented with various sectorwide aid programs. The World Bank actively pushed sector investment programs (SIPs), which have evolved more recently into sector investment and maintenance loans (SIMs) (Denning 1994, Jones and Lawson 2000). All these programs are designed to reintegrate donor activities in a coherent government-planning framework to make aid-supported programs more "owned" by the government. In the ideal sectorwide aid program, the government and donors agree on a sectoral strategy, embodied in a set of policies, a plan, and a budget for the sector. All the donors then contribute funds to the government to implement the strategy. The donors continue their support as long as the government sticks to the agreement.

The most comprehensive current attempt to promote the ownership imperative has been the Poverty Reduction Strategy Papers (PRSP) approach. The World Bank developed this approach in the late 1990s and has since aggressively promoted it (Booth 2001, World Bank 2003a, Eberlei 2001, IDA and IMF 2002). PRSPs have been started in dozens of low-income countries following much the same logic, in which the donors agree with the government on a coherent, multipronged national poverty reduction strategy. The government is encouraged to promote a highly participatory process of decision making as it elaborates this strategy. The donors are then invited to help the government implement the strategy with a variety of more or less integrated activities. The Bank itself prepares a country assistance strategy (CAS) on the basis of the PRSP and identifies a certain number of activities to undertake in the country, typically including budget support for the social sectors. The PRSP process has been widely extended in recent years. As of mid-2003, 15 stagnant low-income states had completed a full PRSP process, and Nigeria was the other stagnant low-income state not involved in an ongoing PRSP process (IMF and IDA 2003). Given how comprehensive this coverage is, and the lofty ambitions the IFIs have placed on then, it is worthwhile to ask how the PRSPs have functioned in practice and the extent to which they advance either local or government ownership.

In most low-income countries, PRSPs have become the cornerstone of the relationship between the government and the IFIs. Initially, the IFIs established the PRSP structure to ensure that governments used the resources from debt relief to fund poverty reduction programs. HIPC II debt relief was made contingent on the government's implementation of a PRSP process judged to be satisfactory by the World Bank and the International Monetary Fund (IMF), as was the eligibility of the government for those institutions' lending instruments. For instance, the IMF's Poverty Reduction and Growth Facility (PRGF) loans are now specifically designed to support an ongoing PRSP process. In a logic influenced by the selectivity approach described earlier, governments will get access to more donor resources once they have demonstrated their commitment to poverty reduction, by undertaking a PRSP that the IFIs consider satisfactory.

The ideal versions of sectorwide programming and PRSPs represent a potentially sharp departure from past practices in two ways. First, the process is designed to enhance local ownership since there is an emphasis on participatory decision making in the domestic arena. Second, PRSPs are designed to reduce the proliferation of aid activities and the problem of donor fragmentation by allowing donors to pool funds and engage in more coordinated activities, as defined by the government-developed antipoverty strategy. Ultimately, PRSPs should pave the way to donors pooling their resources for governmental budget support, though this seems far off.

To get a sense of the success of the PRSPs, I first ask, have they reduced donor fragmentation? Second, what is the evidence that they have promoted local and government ownership?

Although it is still too early to tell whether PRSPs will result in less donor fragmentation and greater coordination, early evidence suggests no decline in the number of donors and projects in low-income states. As suggested earlier, the sheer number of donors and aid projects does not appear to be decreasing. More specifically, the presence of a PRSP does not appear to be leading to major changes in how the donors conduct business. Thus, the sector program for health in Ghana, often held up as a highly successful sector program in the context of a PRSP, still did not capture more than a third of donor resources going to the health sector (Eriksson 2001, 18). Outside of the social sectors, the effect of the PRSP is presumably even less conspicuous, while the number of private and nongovernmental aid agencies, which are not involved in these programs, is constantly increasing.

The inability of PRSPs to arrest fragmentation should not be surprising. The World Bank and a small number of like-minded bilateral donors have led the PRSP process. Indeed, the Bank hesitates to get involved in any programmatic effort in which it is not the lead donor (Jones 1997). In most cases, IFI lending has been the foundation of the donor effort in support of the strategy that is elaborated. The Bank has also dominated the policy dialogue on which the PRSP process is based. The main bilateral donors have then been invited to contribute to the process. While not openly rejecting the process, most donors believe they can accommodate their traditional aid approach to the new system without major changes. As a semiofficial Japanese response to the PRSP makes clear, not all Japanese aid will be integrated into the PRSP, because "some priority areas for assistance identified by Japan's ODA Country Policy do not correspond to those contained in the PRSP" (Institute for International Cooperation [IFIC] and Japan International Cooperation Agency [JICA] 2001, 5). Like most donors, Japan establishes its own country strategy to direct its aid to any given country and does not necessarily take into account the PRSP until relatively late in its aid programming. In any event, like the old five-year plans of the 1960s and 1970s, PRSP documents are broad statements of development intent, and it is pretty easy for the donors to justify already-programmed projects in terms of language in the document.

Table 3.2 suggests this problem exists in most of the stagnant low-income states. Nine donors can claim to be the leading donor in one of the stagnant low-income states, while the Bank is the top donor in only nine of the 26 countries. Japan and the United States, two donors not all that receptive to the PRSP process, are the top donors in six countries, while the Bank is not even one of the top three donors in four countries. Moreover, even if the Bank can get the top three donors to follow its lead on the PRSP process, on average the top three donors only account for two-thirds of the aid going to the country.

Even bilateral donors that are committed to the PRSP may end up contributing to greater fragmentation. In some cases, donors contribute to the resulting sector programs in a more or less coordinated manner, though even donor agencies fully integrated into sector programming apparently continue to do their own monitoring and evaluation of their aid, typically as mandated by their own government. More often, in any event, donors contribute separate independent projects to the PRSP. In practice, program aid usually constitutes a small proportion of most donors' overall aid program in the country, and a number of donors have chosen to disregard the sector aid program framework entirely, because of policy differences, interagency rivalries, or because they find it hard to reconcile their different aid granting procedures and time tables. Some donors have simply not accepted the approach; for instance, USAID has not participated in any sector programs, largely because it has not been able to reconcile them with its own programming framework. Thus, while

Table 3.2 Top three donors of gross ODA, 2000–01 average

Recipient country	Top donor			Second donor			Third donor			Share of top 3 donors in total ODA
	Donor	Millions of dollars	Percent of total ODA	Donor	Millions of dollars	Percent of total ODA	Donor	Millions of dollars	Percent of total ODA	
Central African Republic	France	28	37	Japan	19	25	EC	11	15	77
Chad	France	37	24	EC	28	18	IDA	23	15	57
Comoros	France	11	46	IDA	7	29	EC	4	17	92
Gambia, The	IMF	9	18	IDA	9	18	EC	6	12	48
Ghana	IDA	198	31	United Kingdom	89	14	Japan	83	13	58
Guinea	IDA	55	26	France	40	19	United States	32	15	60
Guinea-Bissau	EC	18	26	Portugal	14	20	IDA	11	16	62
Kenya	IDA	143	30	Japan	83	17	United Kingdom	67	14	61
Kyrgyzstan	ADB	40	20	IDA	39	20	Japan	35	17	57
Madagascar	IDA	103	30	France	65	19	EC	41	12	61
Malawi	IDA	111	26	United Kingdom	85	20	EC	61	14	60
Mali	IDA	106	30	France	96	27	Netherlands	42	12	69
Mauritania	EC	95	40	IDA	55	23	Japan	32	14	77
Moldova	United States	41	34	IDA	22	18	Netherlands	14	12	64
Mongolia	Japan	95	44	ADB	32	15	Germany	22	10	69

Country	Donor 1	Amount	%	Donor 2	Amount	%	Donor 3	Amount	%	Total %
Nicaragua	Spain	210	28	IDB	91	12	United States	87	12	52
Niger	IDA	70	30	France	50	22	EC	27	12	64
Nigeria	IDA	32	17	United States	29	16	United Kingdom	28	15	48
Pakistan	United States	438	33	IDA	370	28	Japan	246	19	80
São Tomé and Príncipe	Portugal	12	33	EC	6	17	IDA	4	11	61
Senegal	France	160	38	IDA	114	27	Japan	39	9	74
Tanzania	Japan	250	22	United Kingdom	222	20	IDA	150	13	55
Togo	France	33	57	IDA	13	22	Germany	8	1	80
Uzbekistan	Japan	57	34	United States	43	25	Germany	11	7	66
Zambia	IDA	178	30	United Kingdom	96	16	Germany	63	11	57
Zimbabwe	Japan	46	27	United Kingdom	21	16	Denmark	20	12	55
Average			31			20			13	64

ADB = Asian Development Bank
EC = European Commission
IDA = World Bank's International Development Association
IDB = Inter-American Development Bank (Fund for Special Operations)
IMF = International Monetary Fund
ODA = official development assistance

Source: Calculated by author from OECD aid statistics database at www.oecd.org.

USAID officially supports the PRSP process, it is not entirely clear what practical impact this actually has on USAID programming.

In sum, if only a few other donors accept the Bank's leadership in any one sector and the rest continue to pursue their own bilateral programming, sector aid programs amount to little more than another parallel management structure and do not promote local ownership of the policy outcomes.

Have the PRSPs altered the donor-recipient relationship and promoted greater ownership? In fact, the objectives of the PRSPs have evolved over time, in relation to ownership. The emphasis on government ownership has tended to recede in favor of participatory aims. Greater involvement of civil society has been viewed as essential to the welfare and poverty reduction objectives that are central to PRSPs. The implicit logic of these programs is that participatory processes will inform and strengthen governmental resolve to implement the programs. As a result, much more attention and resources are now devoted to the expansion of participation than to the ability of governments to integrate and coordinate donor activities. In this sense, the PRSP process does appear to be a genuinely novel approach to aid. It is true, as many critics have noted, that the process is less participatory than consultative: Case studies of ongoing PRSPs in the stagnant low-income states (Dante et al. 2003, Evans and Ngalwea 2003, Jenkins and Tsoka 2003) suggest that the typical mechanism for participation is public presentations of the PRSP to nongovernmental groups. The extent of actual give and take between actors and the extent to which civil society actually has an input into the final policy statement is not clear. As Jenkins and Tsoka (2003, 208) make clear about Malawi, the participatory processes do not necessarily increase the accountability of government: In a statement that could well apply to most stagnant low-income states, they write that "it is extremely unlikely that this will result in the emergence of domestic political leverage sufficient to hold government (or donors) accountable for commitments undertaken in the PRSP formulation process. Civil society remains extremely weak and fragmented, and government highly suspicious of the more vocal elements within its ranks." However, there is no gainsaying that the novelty of any type of public presentation of policy in what have been closed decision-making systems is a significant step forward and one of the real achievements of the PRSP process.

PRSPs have been much less successful in terms of promoting government ownership, because they have largely failed to change the nature of the relationship between governments and donors. First, the PRSP process is entirely an invention of the donor community, even if actual PRSPs are homegrown. Recipients would never undertake PRSPs if they were not a condition to access debt relief funds and more IFI lending. In this sense, PRSPs have merely replaced other IFI-driven processes that are imposed on recipient countries.

This is fairly clear if the scope and substantive focus of the PRSPs are examined. PRSPs have overwhelmingly focused on the social sectors and more specifically on service delivery, which the donors have come to focus on in the last decade. They are much less relevant to other developmental concerns such as capacity building in the core ministerial structures, and they are almost entirely silent on areas such as defense policy, where governments spend a large proportion of their own revenues.

Second, the format of PRSP documents and the types of policies they should include are closely defined by the World Bank, and its monitoring missions make sure countries remain faithful to the vision of PRSPs the Bank has laid out. So, even if the process is participatory and home-grown, the actual policies that emerge from the process are wholly predictable. I have informally asked half a dozen Bank officials with personal experience of PRSPs for examples of PRSPs changing specific Bank policies about given countries in a meaningful manner: Other than alleging a much greater likelihood of long delays in decision making, they have not been able to come up with any specific examples of such policy changes on the part of the Bank.

Third, implementation of donor projects in support of PRSPs often follows old, well-established patterns. For example, donor agencies face real pressure to demonstrate effectiveness to their domestic constituencies and legislative overseers. This leads to evaluations that emphasize short-term, quantifiable results, which are difficult to reconcile with the logic of PRSPs. As a result, the donor presence is often much more intrusive than the architects of these programs envisaged. In a generally positive review of the PRSP process in Uganda, Adam and Gunning (2002, 2050) write that to monitor the program, the donors find themselves "lock[ed] . . . into forms of micromanagement, based around a large number of input and process indicators that did so much to discredit earlier approaches to conditionality." In many cases, the demands of evaluation lead these donors to demand an identifiable, discrete component of the sector program for them to manage and then claim credit for, which in effect brings it back to a set of projects. Note that such a program may still represent a significant step forward, if the government retains an effective overall coordination role and helps promote greater discipline and collaboration among donors.

Moving Away from State-Led Development Strategies

Even as the donor community has concluded that greater government ownership is central to more effective aid, it has sought ways of bypassing central state structures in favor of private and local actors. Another conventional view that gained support in the 1990s has been that less aid should go to the central state and more to nongovernmental actors in the private sector, civil society, and local communities. Somewhat paradoxically, even as the donors have become more demanding of central states in the low-income economies, they have developed the doctrine that fewer resources should go to these central states. Until the early 1990s, aid was overwhelmingly an intergovernmental exchange, and only a minute proportion of aid escaped central governments' control. This pattern was eventually seriously questioned, in large part because of the obvious deficiencies of central governments. The emergence of structural adjustment in the early 1980s coincided with the donor and academic communities sharply criticizing "state-led" development. The World Bank, under the intellectual leadership of Anne Krueger, was particularly important in this evolution. A number of critics have argued with this position, suggesting that the Bank had erred in a neoliberal direction and pointing to a handful of East Asian success stories as evidence of the merits of a highly interventionist central state (Wade 1990, Amsden 1989).

In practice, nonetheless, a large number of new institutional actors have emerged to take resources and attention away from central states. For the donor organizations, the practical dilemmas of how to overcome the legacy of weak indigenous institutions and nondevelopmental governments have largely pushed aside the intellectual debates about long-term development strategies. Donors have always sought viable organizational vehicles with which to deliver services and overcome endemic deficiencies in skilled-staff availability, communications, and infrastructure. The need to move relatively large volumes of aid has led most to favor expedient and short-term solutions to institutional problems. Not having found these vehicles within the state, donors have long turned their attention to other implementation mechanisms available in the short term—from independent project units to parastatals and, in the more recent past, to NGOs (van de Walle and Johnston 1996, Meyer 1992).

In the idealized interpretation of this evolution, particularly the version the donors endorsed, the central state will devolve a number of peripheral tasks—its past performance of which was mediocre anyway—to local governments and the voluntary and private sector. Thus refocused, a leaner and more effective state will emerge. Following standard economic doctrine, for instance, the World Bank's *World Development Report 1997* argues that low-income states should focus on the following "core public goods and services": "A foundation of lawfulness, a stable macro-economy, the rudiments of public health, universal primary education, adequate transport infrastructure, and a minimal safety net" (World Bank 1997; see also Stiglitz 1996).

The donors' dissatisfaction with the central state in low-income countries has led it to promote two new actors: the NGO sector and local government. In both cases, however, the net advantage gained is more modest than often assumed, and the negative impact on the central state's ability to promote development may outweigh any potential benefits.

The NGO Sector

NGOs have benefited from the belief that the private sector is preferable to the public sector and from the view that they are vehicles for democratization. The emergence of the NGO sector is particularly striking. In some low-income countries, NGOs now provide or implement more than a fifth of total aid flows compared with less than 1 percent 15 years ago (Hulme and Edwards 1997, Riddell and Robinson 1995). In certain sectors of activity, such as relief operations, they have become the dominant players, directly involved in the disbursement of over two-thirds of all funds ("Sins of the Secular Missionaries," *The Economist*, January 29, 2000). By one estimate, foundations and private Americans donate between $10 billion and $17 billion a year to development activities in Third World countries, and these totals appear to be rapidly increasing even as official aid has stopped increasing (Whittle 2002). Current debates within the aid community commonly advocate the expansion of aid efforts filtered through the NGOs (Clark 1991, 2003).

On the other hand, the amount and type of aid that can be channeled through NGOs is probably limited by the nature of NGOs in the low-income economies. They may have a comparative advantage in service delivery and managing intensive microactivities, but they are less likely to be effective for large public works or national-level activities. Donors are discovering that they quickly exhaust the low absorptive capacity of the NGO sector, unless they are willing to undertake substantial and time-consuming institution building. NGO projects are typically management-intensive; yet, most donors have not realized the managerial implications of decentralizing aid programs successfully. Instead, donors appear content to base aid to nongovernmental actors within their traditional administrative frameworks, leading to a high proportion of implementation problems (e.g., Bossuyt 1997).

It is convenient for donors to treat NGOs as little more than a cost-effective service provider for their activities in certain sectors. The donors save money and avoid having to address implementation difficulties, while nevertheless retaining ultimate control over activities. In authoritarian or corrupt regimes, delegating aid to NGOs allows donors to claim not to be supporting the government. Yet, the use of NGOs as donor service providers appears strikingly similar to the independent project units of the past and—as with—it is difficult to see how NGOs can contribute to long-term institution building outside of the state. While many NGOs have been able to forge deep links within the societies in which they operate, a large number are entirely reliant for their existence on the support of a small number of donors. In 2000, for instance, *The Economist* reported that only 9 of the 120 local NGOs in Kenya were not entirely financed by Western donors ("Sins of the Secular Missionaries," *The Economist*, January 29, 2000). These NGOs have apparently discovered that it is a lot easier to raise funding from rich foreign donors than from extremely poor local communities. Whatever their discourse and original ambitions, such NGOs have no existence outside of the official aid system. This may explain why the empirical evidence suggests that NGO-implemented aid may suffer from worse sustainability problems than traditional aid (Riddell and Robinson 1995).

The absence of NGOs with dues-paying members has two implications. First, many of the organizations that have emerged are unusually reliant on external support. In many countries, the recent explosion of NGOs is in part the result of donor support (Dicklitch 1998). Donors view NGOs as cost-effective implementation vehicles for development activities and are willing to finance their expansion. Thomas Bierschenk and Jean Pierre Olivier de Sardan (1997, 447) note that many village organizations in the Central African Republic's countryside "are often established in the hope of receiving development aid, and apart from the fact that a sizeable number exist merely on paper, in all cases the meager results achieved seldom justified the scope of the funding provided by the donors. Like the development organizations which are behind their creation, these groups concentrate their efforts on inputs and not outputs: the procurement of subsidies as opposed to production of any kind."

Bierschenk and Olivier de Sardan's pessimism notwithstanding, reliance on donors does not preclude effectiveness and is not necessarily a bad thing (Hulme and Edwards 1997); in time, some of these donor creations may institutionalize and gain independence. But the absence of revenue generation often results in NGOs that are accountable to the donors rather than to their members and that follow a donor agenda (Van Rooy 1998).

Second, in the absence of dues-paying members, these organizations are much more vulnerable to being hijacked by the ambitions and dishonesty of individual entrepreneurs (Bratton 1994). Accusations of corruption and fraud by NGO managers are endemic in many countries, and the facts often belie the argument that the NGO sector is necessarily more virtuous than the public sector. Indigenous NGOs in low-income countries find themselves in an environment that is extremely propitious for abuses. Their governance structures rarely provide for mechanisms of accountability for their managers, since they often do not have dues-paying members, an autonomous board of directors, or an effective state fiscal agency to monitor them.

Decentralization and Local Government

The growing attention to *decentralization* in the stagnant low-income states emanates largely from the same logic. Donors increasingly view local governments as potentially more effective than central governments at promoting development and more democratic because local governments are more accountable and responsive to the citizenry. Accountable and pluralistic local governments could assist, harness, and coordinate the rich resources posited to exist at the local level. The donors have argued that decentralization is a key component of their efforts to promote democratization of political life and to improve the efficiency of public services (Manor 1999). As a result, most donors have enthusiastically promoted national policies of decentralization and administrative devolution, and the 1990s witnessed efforts to implement decentralization in virtually every one of the stagnant low-income states.

In **Mali,** for example, laws passed in 1995 created 701 rural and urban *communes* to replace the old system of 270 *arrondissements*, and these communes will eventually have responsibilities for primary education, health care, local road construction and maintenance, public transportation, water distribution, and sports and cultural events. (In addition to the 701 communes, the reform creates 52 *cercles* or counties and eight regions; see CDIE 1998.)

In **Burkina Faso**, the government created the Commission Nationale de Décentralisation (CND) in 1993 to promote decentralization. An ambitious program was then defined, which created 33 municipalities in the country's principal towns and will eventually result in up to 500 municipal councils all over the country.

In **Niger** in the early 1990s, the new democratic government officially committed itself to an ambitious decentralization program. The end of the Third Republic and the installation of a military government did not end the decentralization momentum, even if one definite motivation for decentralization was to promote greater political pluralism in the countryside (Tidjani Alou 1998). Following local elections in 1999, some 994 municipal representatives and 787 communal officials were to be freely elected, suggesting the program's ambitious dimensions.

In **Pakistan**, the government initiated a decentralization process in 1999, which calls for the creation of 6,455 local self-governments, including 92 districts, 4 city districts, 307 *tehsil* governments, and 6,022 union councils. Eventually, the government foresees extensive fiscal decentralization, but in the short term, the biggest implication is the creation of local elected officials, which the government hopes will improve service delivery (World Bank 2002c, 9–11).

What are the prospects for these new local governments? In most low-income countries, decentralization has foreseen the transfer of certain responsibilities to the local level, and communities have been given new fiscal prerogatives. But very little systematic evidence is available on how much has already been achieved. Evidence exists of significant fiscal devolution to primary cities. An interesting USAID study of decentralization in Mali (CDIE 1998) also suggests that the process has proceeded furthest for large towns but notes some uncertainty from the outset, even for towns, about the extent of fiscal devolution implied by the creation of these new local administrations.

The situation is somewhat different in the countryside, where it is usually quite premature to speak of significant devolution at this point. There is anecdotal evidence of newly elected officials in rural communities undertaking relatively bold initiatives on their own, usually in the realm of small village-level infrastructure or health and education services. In the absence of statistics, it is impossible to tell how significant a trend these experiences represent. The evidence does suggest that donors who are willing to finance decentralization activities drive much of the devolution. Central governments have more ambiguous attitudes toward reforms that would inevitably take away resources and discretionary power if fully implemented. On the one hand, in the current fiscal crisis and given their own lamentable record of providing services to populations, they are unlikely to turn down donor resources that pay for any level of government. Moreover, many face subnational pressures to decentralize authority (Ndegwa 2002, 1). On the other hand, they are unlikely to view the giving up of power with equanimity. Plenty of case studies suggest that whatever government impetus officially given to the process, in practice the central ministerial services often resist giving up long-standing prerogatives and discretion (e.g., CDIE 1998, Lambright 2003).

The absence of local revenues underlines the critical role of the donors in empowering local authorities. The IMF unfortunately does not provide any recent systematic data on revenues disaggregated by level of government in the poorest economies. Anecdotal data from a number of low-income countries nonetheless suggest how small a proportion of overall funding is likely to come from local sources. Thus, in 1991, Kenya's central government collected 98.3 percent of national taxes and local governments only 1.7 percent, despite a relatively long established tradition of local administration and much stronger municipal government than in most low-income states (Shome 1995, 250). Among low-income countries, the highest levels of local revenue generation may well be in Uganda, where it has been the government's priority for over a decade. Yet, Gina Lambright (2003) reports that even the most capable Ugandan district governments managed to finance well under 10 percent of their costs from self-generated revenues. In time, perhaps local authorities will be able to generate revenues to finance their activities; for now, they are heavily reliant on donors.

In sum, the search for alternatives to corrupt and incompetent central governments in low-income states has led donors to seek alternative mechanisms for aid implementation. The focus, unfortunately, has been more on instruments with which to move money rapidly rather than on the much more difficult task of building viable institutions outside of the central state. The donors are likely to discover that it is no easier to build capacity within local government than it was in the central state apparatus. In practice, many of the flaws of aid dependency witnessed in the central state are being reproduced in the new institutions. Once again, these problems are terribly exacerbated in the poorest economies. Where the central state is weakest, the local government and civil society are also likely to be weakest.

4

Understanding the Failures of Aid Reform

Why have various donor attempts to reform aid failed to improve the growth prospects of the aid-dependent stagnant low-income states (SLIS)? Of course, many in the aid community sincerely believe that ongoing reform efforts are substantially transforming aid, thus allowing it to promote real poverty alleviation and growth in the near future. In retrospect, not much progress was made on key issues during several previous reform periods, but perhaps this time, reform will have a profound effect.

My skepticism is in part inductive: As I argued in the preceding chapter, largely unresolved contradictions exist between the different current donor reform objectives. Achievement of some objectives is likely to undermine the achievement of others. Some of these reforms cannot succeed without coordination among the donors and more careful prioritization of reforms. Even if they do, the empirical reality on the ground suggests that the current reforms have failed to address two of the central reasons for failure in the past: absence of aid coordination and inability of aid to promote significant improvements of state capacity in the stagnant low-income states. Chapter 3 showed in particular that the introduction of sector program aid and of the Poverty Reduction Strategy Papers (PRSP) approach did not reduce the large number of distinct donor activities in low-income countries, though it was one of their explicit objectives. In chapters 4 and 5 I relate these problems to the limited effects of recent reforms.

A second cause for skepticism regarding current reform proposals is more deductive: Most of the recipient governments have not changed, most of the donor organizations remain the same, and the incentives governing relations between them have changed only marginally. With so much left unchanged, where will the impetus for change come from? In the final chapter, I examine the issue of incentives, particularly on the donor side.

Contradictions among Donor Objectives

The three main recent donor objectives—selectivity, ownership, and larger role of private and local actors—discussed in chapter 3 all have compelling individual justifications. In practice, however, unresolved tensions exist between them. First, there is considerable tension between the current ownership proposals and the new emphasis on delegating aid implementation to organizations outside of the central state. Many of these organizations have emerged in response to the perceived deficiencies of the state. The spirit of NGO-government relations is often adversarial, as both the NGOs and government compete for the same finite donor resources. Indeed, when donors support independent organizations, state institutions lose out on multiple fronts. Trained manpower drains away from the ministries, lured by the considerably higher salaries that donors and NGOs offer. The state's structures are in turn marginal to developmental activities and lose credibility with local populations, who turn away from administrations without resources. Having lost their core functions and often woefully underfunded, these ministries are more likely to engage in nondevelopmental activities such as rent-seeking.

Donors invariably preach the existence of a developmental complementarity between state and nonstate actors, but to state agents, the competition for donor support more typically feels like a zero-sum game, with a winner and a loser. Why should they collaborate with organizations that are taking away their primary source of development funding? These problems are particularly acute in the stagnant low-income states, where the budget constraints are worse and the level of professionalism within the civil service the lowest.

Recipient governments are unlikely to feel committed to aid resources that have been taken away and decentralized to multiple local actors over which they have no control. Advocates of NGO assistance insist that they promote the commitment of local stakeholders to development even if the government is left uninvolved. In some cases, this is surely true, even if many NGOs get the overwhelming majority of their operating capital from donor projects and thus are only rarely truly independent, driven by community concerns, or both. But as Judith Tendler (1997) remarks of northeastern Brazil, it is wrong to assume that NGOs are necessarily closer to their stakeholders than democratic, accountable, public services can be. Certainly the mediocre sustainability record of

NGO assistance points to the limits of this stakeholder support. If the government will eventually be asked to come in and supply the needed finances once the donors pull out, donors need to think much more carefully about how to promote NGO-government links during the project cycle.

NGO aid is also overwhelmingly extended as traditional project aid. Since the NGOs derive their strength directly from their small size and independence, it is not clear how they should be reconciled with the stronger national planning and budgeting processes also currently advocated by the donors. It is not unusual for a stagnant low-income state's health or education sector to benefit from projects from a dozen donors, over half of which will be independent of the central government and involving perhaps that many NGOs, project units, and local authorities. In practice, all over the low-income developing world, this proliferation of actors seriously compromises the government's ability to undertake even minimal regulatory and development planning functions.

A second problematic tension exists between the donors' ownership and selectivity objectives. In practice, the move from conditionality to selectivity often entails a degree of *ventriloquism*, in which the donors make clear what their policy expectations are, and governments understand what they need to say and do in order to get the foreign assistance. As Gerry Helleiner (2002, 255) has put it, "some donors seem to believe that ownership exists when recipients do what we want them to do but they do so voluntarily." If governments are free to own only the set of policies that the donors have already decided upon, the real degree of ownership that the new approach generates will not differ from the old conditionality dynamics. In the current PRSP process, for instance, the recipient government is *required* to undertake a participatory process that involves consultations with nongovernmental stakeholders regarding the program. Not only are the stakeholders often aid-dependent local NGOs but also the donors carefully vet the set of poverty reduction measures that make up the program, and the conclusions of the participatory process are circumscribed to policy outcomes that the donors support.

Thus, despite the ownership rhetoric, PRSPs often voice a government intention to address a detailed list of policy issues, which donors have suggested if not wholly determined. PRSP implementation is clearly donor-driven, with its large contingent of foreign expertise and aid-sponsored fora such as the Consultative Group meetings or the roundtables typically setting the program's parameters. It is therefore not clear that the implementation of selectivity actually decreases the scope and intensity of donor interference in day-to-day decision making, which was also the hallmark of conditionality, or that it promotes a sense of government ownership over the program.

Donor attempts to move to selectivity strategies, with instruments such as the PRSPs, continue to result in dysfunctional goal displacement by aid-dependent governments, whose policy-making objective is no longer to promote internal capacity or goals such as economic growth but instead to please the donors so that they will provide aid. This kind of goal displacement is especially obvious in the aid-dependent stagnant low-income states, where the main purpose of large components of the central state is to extract resources from donors: large travel budgets exclusively to attend donor functions, or a well-funded department within each ministry to interact with the donors, all of which often attract the best civil servants. In sum, national development policymaking becomes subsumed in various ways under the relationship with the donors.

Most troubling, the PRSPs are rarely fully integrated into the national budgetary process, which the PRSPs often supersede in importance in the donors' eyes. Donor evaluations of PRSPs (IDA and IMF 2002, 21) call for better integration of the national budget and the PRSP process. But the only conceivable reason governments undertake a PRSP is to get access to donor resources, so it is hard to see how the PRSP process will not take some attention and resources away from the budgetary process. If they are perfectly integrated, one is redundant; if they are not, then the PRSP can serve only to weaken the legitimacy and efficacy of the budget.

Under pressures from Western NGOs, official donors have implicitly defined participation largely in terms of nongovernmental actors within civil society. One consequence is that PRSPs are very rarely formally debated in the national legislature, even in democratic countries with competitively elected legislatures (IDA and IMF 2002, 9; Booth 2001). Thus, even if senior officials "own" a program, the country's elected representatives may know little about its details. Uganda is often viewed as an exemplar of this new, more participatory process (e.g., Adam and Gunning 2002), but my November 2000 interviews with a dozen parliamentary backbenchers in Kampala revealed that they knew little about the ongoing PRSP process and had not been involved in the program's design. Revealingly, several referred to the PRSP as "the World Bank program."

The tension between the new selectivity discourse and ownership is particularly striking in much of the literature on European aid. The European Commission in Brussels is very keen to oppose the conditionality of the Washington institutions in favor of its own more progressive conception of a "partnership" between Europe and the African, Caribbean, and Pacific (ACP) states, which it claims promotes local ownership. During the 1990s, however, the Commission increased the conditions in its grant making under pressure from member governments to improve the impact of its aid. Publicly it has tried hard to avoid the language of conditionality to justify this evolution. These are not conditions, the Commission argues, they are "criteria of good management," which are only normal in a "partnership" that is "adult, rigorous, open, without compromise. . ." (Frisch 1997, 64). The distinction between "criteria among adults" and conditions will be lost on governments. They will surely notice that the Commission's rhetoric belies the fact that it is increasing its interference in their internal decision making and enforcing distinctions between aid activities and government activities.

It is revealing in this respect that donor discussions of coordination invariably describe it as a process of donor coordination rather than government coordination of aid resources, which is what is really at stake. William Easterly's (2003) description of donor coordination as an attempt to forge a donor cartel is suggestive. Too often, the main motivation for coordination is the enforcement of conditionality, rather than the promotion of more efficient government management of the aid process. Particularly in low-income countries with extensive governance problems, donors feel like they need to present a common front to the government in order to convince the government to undertake certain policy reforms. The donor discourse invariably frames the issue of coordination as a matter of getting the government from point A to point B. But the broader and more important case for coordination is that it achieves the rationalization of aid resources and their insertion into a coherent development strategy that the government fully owns. This more ambitious form of coordination puts the government at the center of the development process, where it ought to be (van de Walle and Johnston 1996). Indeed, if and when governments coordinate the aid effort as part of their own coherent development effort, the evidence suggests that problems of local ownership of aid largely disappear. Governments are more committed to aid activities and more likely to be able and willing to sustain them following the end of donor resources.

The aid experience of Botswana, one of the poorest countries at the time of its independence, is a case in point. A number of observers of the Botswana experience (Lewis 1993; Lister 1991; Maipose, Somolekae, and Johnston 1996; Harvey 1992; Acemoglu, Johnson, and Robinson 2003) have remarked upon the degree to which the government of Botswana is unique in Africa in how it took control of the aid process right after independence and made sure it was integrated into its own national budgeting and planning procedures. These observers argue that Botswana was able to refuse donor proposals that did not fit well into its own priorities and insisted on the tailoring of donor activities to the government's way of doing things. It helped that Botswana's economy thrived in the decades after independence, thanks in part to the discovery of diamonds, and that the country's macroeconomic stability helped avoid the kind of crisis management prevalent in other aid-dependent low-income states. But the important point is that Botswana embarked on this course at its independence, when this success was far from assured. Several of its neighbors also had substantial mineral wealth; some enjoyed robust growth in the years immediately following independence. In its careful management of national diamond resources and its ability to maintain macrostability, the Botswana government demonstrated the same strengths it exhibited in its management of aid resources. Success in one area helped ensure success in others.

How can the donors encourage the emergence of more such proactive governments that take the lead in aid programs and force greater discipline on the current system? Despite all the rhetoric from the donors on this issue, there is little evidence at present that they are willing to change the way they do business to allow such governments to emerge. Nor is there much evidence that many recipient governments of low-income economies have the capacity or the inclination to grasp this leadership role. Until these programs are much more firmly embedded within the government's own planning and budgeting activities, it is hard to see how ownership will ever be completely genuine.

Why Is Institutional Capacity So Elusive?

The failure of various donor reform initiatives continues to be blamed on problems of state capacity, yet it seems that enhancing state capacity has been a top donor priority for several decades. Time and again, good donor intentions for the low-income states founder because of capacity problems. For instance, the main obstacle to making progress on local ownership of aid has often been problems linked to low capacity. The World Bank itself has noted in several reports that the PRSP programs have been the least successful in low-income states because of problems of capacity (e.g., World Bank 2003a). The current difficulties with decentralization and promoting local government similarly have been related primarily to capacity issues. Why can't donors promote institutional capacity more effectively?

There are several relevant issues here. First, economic instability and macroeconomic disequilibria are almost certainly extremely harmful to institutional capacity. Governments that are in crisis management mode because they cannot maintain fiscal balance are more likely to take expedient shortcuts that undermine capacity, such as the accumulation of civil service salary arrears. The fact that most of the stagnant low-income states have been in macroeconomic crisis repeatedly over the last two decades is a big reason why efforts to promote state capacity during this period have been unsuccessful. The longer the period of fiscal crisis, the more problems of institutional capacity accumulate and worsen. Stop-gap measures and expedient solutions work in the short run but not over multiple budget cycles. In many low-income countries, the decades of underspending on maintenance and public-sector infrastructure exact an important cost today.

Second, as suggested earlier, *many donor practices actually undermine government capacity.* The predilection for uncoordinated project aid constitutes a massive managerial burden on low-capacity governments. Qualified staff spend too much time negotiating and managing relations with the donor agencies, which detracts from the time they could spend actually promoting development. In what are very thin public administrations, the endless flow of project identification, monitoring and evaluation missions, consultative group meetings, and various sorts of donor roundtables or consultations represent a substantial time commitment (Berg 1997). In addition, the lure of donor resources and the central role of the donors in the recipient countries mean that the most ambitious and best staff are often placed in the units that are in charge of donor relations. A form of bureaucratic rent-seeking can be associated with foreign aid: local bureaucrats devoting their useful skills and time not to promote development but to access the various perks that the relationship with the donors can provide—the Consultative Group meeting in Paris, with its generous per diem; the three-week training course in Washington; the project car; and so on. In each case, the opportunity cost involved for local developmental capacity is significant. In this sense, and somewhat paradoxically, aid often weakens the technocratic element in low-income countries to the benefit of clientelistic tendencies. A multitude of donors undertaking numerous ad hoc development activities outside of main government channels undermine government efforts to enforce rules of bureaucratic propriety and transparency. With multiple parallel budgeting possibilities, a lower proportion of domestic expenditures is scrutinized, and it is harder for governments to prevent abuses (see Bräutigam [2000] and van de Walle [2001] for multiple examples).

Similarly, the donors have continued to express a preference for long-term foreign experts in the field, despite the fact that few evaluations have found them to be cost-effective in promoting institutional capacity (Berg 1993). No recent estimates exist of the total number of foreign experts in the low-income countries, but little evidence suggests they have declined in number or cost; John Cohen (1992, 493) cites the number of 100,000 foreign experts in Africa in 1989, at a cost of $4 billion and amounting to 35 percent of the official development assistance (ODA) to the region. For his part, Elliott Berg (1993, 72) argues the number is "closer to 40,000 than to 80,000." In any event, the opportunity cost is huge. Berg (p. 14) notes that the cost of foreign experts in Tanzania in the late 1980s amounted to twice the cost of the entire civil service payroll. It is a particularly ironic situation for countries that continue to lose many of their best-trained professionals to the West.

As Cohen (1992) and others have argued, the donors have maintained their predilection for these expensive foreign experts because they serve as useful intermediaries between the aid organization and the local project environment. Donor organizations continue to ensure that many experts are hired—even if their development impact is minimal—to make sure donor conditions are met by governments that are not considered trustworthy or so that donor projects are managed in a way that is acceptable to donor bureaucracies. Foreign experts "speak the same language" as the donor organizations; they provide useful links to the consulting firms, universities, and think tanks that are the donors' leading constituency. As a result, their numbers remain stable, despite their enormous cost and ambiguous impact on institution building.

Third, donors have in fact paid inadequate attention to the issues of institution building. This assertion will not be popular in the donor community. It is true that the donor discourse about the importance of institution building has changed in recent years. The World Bank's *World Development Report 1997* on the state signaled the Bank's new attitude toward these issues. Berg (2000) notes that the 1990s witnessed a renewed effort to improve the public management capacities of recipient governments: Many of these efforts were led by the World Bank, which had overseen more than 200 public expenditure reform operations by 1998; Berg estimates that by the late 1990s, public-sector management programs totaled over 5 percent of total World Bank lending (Berg 2000, 290–91; see also Arndt 2000).

Yet Barbara Nunberg's 1997 assertion that World Bank attempts to address issues of government capacity were ineffective because "the skills, resources, and organizational focus brought to bear on these problems . . . have been inadequate" remains true and could be extended to most of the other official donors. To promote other donor objectives, efforts to improve capacity are typically implemented in the context of specific donor projects. Thus, a donor establishes a project to increase the education ministry's capacity to improve primary education in the context of a project to expand the rural population's access to education. This *projectization* of capacity building gives it an ad hoc nature, which ensures its limited and often unsustainable impact. Donors have rarely addressed the underlying reasons for low state capacity. Once the education project is finished, the government has few incentives to maintain the project's expensive capacity-building unit. The state of the civil service in most of the stagnant low-income states testifies to this inattention, as described earlier. Despite the impressive rhetoric about promoting ownership, most civil services have been treated with benign neglect: They have been allowed to be politicized, accumulate salary arrears, and evolve increasingly poor working conditions.

Fourth, and related, donors continue to act as if institutional capacity were exogenous to the governments to which they provide assistance. In other words, low institutional capacity is viewed in much the same way as donors view low levels of rainfall. It is a given, over which the local government has little control. The solution to low levels of precipitation is investing in irrigation; the solution to low capacity is foreign expertise and training programs. In fact, 50 years after the end of colonialism, capacity should be viewed as endogenous, a product of the history and current politics of the recipient government. As suggested earlier, the day-to-day problems of low capacity are due in large part to structural dynamics, which lead governments to underinvest in capacity building. Capacity in the civil service declines over time, despite the ever-growing number of graduates, for a complex set of reasons that includes the politicization of recruitment and promotions, the absence of an independent civil service commission, and annual budgets that systematically underfinance recurrent supplies and services. National accounting and statistical services worsen year after year despite the exponential growth in the number of civil servants with technical skills, in part because corrupt governments are very ambivalent about precise and transparent public information systems and make little effort to promote them. As a World Bank report noted blandly about Haiti recently, "the virtual absence of a national procurement system...[makes] misprocurement likely" (World Bank 2002b, 4).

What does this mean for donor programs? Foremost, it means that the contemporary capacity-building efforts are largely, sisyphean, doomed to fail. The problem is not technical—it is not equivalent to the problem of building the perfect irrigation pump. Instead, it is about changing the current incentives that are leading local institutions to under-invest in capacity.

Donor efforts to improve expenditure management provide a good example of these dynamics (Lister and Stevens 1992, Campos and Pradhan 1996). Half a dozen generations of attempts have been made to improve public expenditure management in the poorest countries, from teams of foreign experts in the ministries of finance to the alphabet soup of reform programs promoted by the international financial institutions (IFIs) in the 1980s and 1990s: the public investment program (PIP), the public expenditure reviews (PERS), and most recently the integrated financial management information systems (IFMIS). Both the Bank and the Fund have come to recognize the limited effectiveness of each of these reforms (Berg 2000). They embodied several different reform strategies and management philosophies. Some avowedly sought to increase donor control of expenditure management. More recently, the donor philosophy has been to seek to improve "local ownership" of the management process. Here again, the early signs are of disappointing results. As discussed in chapter 3, problems of ownership and institutional capacity have bedeviled each generation of donor efforts.

One obvious common shortcoming of all of these programs is that they fail to increase the public accountability of expenditure management institutions. Under the impulse of the Jubilee 2000 movement, tentative steps have been taken to improve vertical accountability of governments in how they spend the revenues derived through debt relief. In a number of cases, the donors have provided support to local NGOs to monitor the extent and quality of social-sector expenditure. In Uganda, under pressure from NGOs and donors, the government has been pressured to post on school doors the amount of money disbursed to the headmaster, in order to reduce the diversion of money from its stated purpose (World Bank 2003b, 31). This often-told anecdote suggests governments are more sensitive to NGO and donor criticism of corruption. There is no evidence, however, that SLIS governments have responded with increased internal capacity to fight corruption.

Moreover, little or no attention has been paid to improving horizontal accountability, which is another key dimension of any accountability strategy. In particular, in their attempts to improve public expenditure processes, donors and governments alike have almost entirely ignored the strengthening of the legislature's ability to monitor the public expenditure process and sanction abuses (Lienert and Sarraf 2001).

Unchanging Donor Incentives

Why don't current reforms get at key issues? The absence of aid coordination has been noted for a long time, with little effect. Every major study of aid has bemoaned the slow pace of capacity building. The central role of ownership has similarly been a constant theme of aid effectiveness debates. Yet each of these problems persists, and it seems like the current donor initiatives have not made much progress on these key issues. Discussions of the difficulty of change tend to put the focus on conditions within the aid-recipient countries themselves. Particularly in the low-income states, the donors tend to blame the absence of progress on local problems of capacity and governance. Clearly, it is important not to underestimate the difficulties of promoting change in poor countries; yet an aid system that fails to work in the poorest countries is clearly failing in some fundamental manner. I argue that the main difficulty is changing how the donor agencies themselves operate. Indeed, proposals for internal reform of donor agencies are singularly missing from the current debates. Yet, so many of the problems of aid have to do with its organization on the donor side.

There is little denying that reforming foreign aid is a popular pastime in the aid business. The last half-century has witnessed half a dozen authoritative studies of foreign aid, each of which has suggested ways to reform the implementation of aid programs. Every new administrator at the US Agency for International Development (USAID) and every incoming president of the World Bank undertakes an expensive and disruptive institutional reorganization, with the official objective, among others, of making the institution's aid more effective.

What has been the impact of all this "reform mongering"? The *allocation* of foreign aid has significantly changed in recent years. As discussed earlier, governance and policy criteria have increased in importance in recent years. Governments in low-income countries now worry that their policy and governance deficiencies will result in a lower volume of international assistance. Their newfound willingness to face their voters in regular elections and other examples of political liberalization (freedom of the press and associational freedoms) have many causes, but the need to assuage the donors is a clear one. Of course, the governments' tendency to limit the impact of political liberalization and the continuing predilection for authoritarian practices should alert one to the limits of the new dispensation. As argued earlier, it remains relatively easy to assuage the donors.

Moreover, much less real change has taken place in the *implementation* of foreign aid programs. The basic model of implementation—with its reliance on multiple uncoordinated projects, foreign expertise, and little local ownership—remains largely unchanged despite the new rhetoric and some sincere attempts to bring about change. Three sets of factors represent the biggest constraints on changing aid: bureaucratic politics within the donor agencies, absence of donor accountability, and the nature of external domestic pressures on aid agencies.

Bureaucratic Politics in Donor Agencies

Many of the problems identified in the previous paragraphs have proven difficult to resolve because of dynamics within the aid bureaucracy. The failure of conditionality is thus often quite rightly ascribed to the pressures in aid bureaucracies to "move the money." Promotions reward program officers who manage large portfolios rather than those who manage successful portfolios. Departments lose the budgetary allocations they fail to spend, so they have an incentive to make sure project and program funding is allocated and spent. In the 1990s, different observers argued that the pressure to spend money substantially weakened conditionality, since governments continued to receive money even if they did not meet the conditions. The evidence reported earlier suggests that budgetary pressures did lead the donors to exhibit somewhat more discipline in the more recent past. With aid being cut back, donors were forced to make more careful judgments about aid allocation, and there is some evidence that this did lead to greater discipline and allocation selectivity. Still, the bureaucratic incentives faced by the staff in donor agencies continue to promote an aid implementation process that emphasizes rapid disbursement.

Similarly, despite long-standing evidence that the absence of donor coordination has undermined aid effectiveness, the truth is that remarkably little progress has been made on donor coordination issues during the last decade. It is important to realize that the failure of donor coordination is almost entirely due to bureaucratic resistance within donor agencies. Each agency is happy to gain greater discretion over other agencies' programs and resources in the name of coordination but unwilling to give up significant power over its own. As one early analysis offered, donors love to coordinate, but they hate being coordinated (Whittington and Calhoun 1988). Coordinating brings with it additional discretion and power, while being coordinated means less of these things and so organizations resist it. To be fair, real coordination would impose significant costs on each agency, as each would have to make significant adjustments in its programming cycle, procurement, auditing, and evaluation procedures in order to align them with those of other donors. Coordination also implies greater specialization, where each donor would focus on a more narrow set of activities in which it has a comparative advantage. This, too, would be onerous for agencies, as it would mean some reorganization of staff and resources.

Moreover, donor bureaucracies have undermined their own attempts at reforming the modalities of aid because of their desire to maintain operational control of their activities. Thus, the predilection for foreign experts is due less to developmental concerns than to the desire to have a trustworthy intermediary in the field who will report to the donor agency and serve its interests, not least because he or she is generally dependent on the goodwill of the agency for continued employment. Moreover, foreign experts know the agency and its procedures and can be expected to fill out the required agency reports in the donor's national language.

Similarly, the reticence of many aid agencies to move toward program aid can be understood as motivated by the desire to retain control over aid implementation in the field. The advantage of the project structure, for all of its faults, is that it provides donor agency staff with maximum discretion and autonomy during the implementation phase. The independent project unit can make its own rules and need not pay attention to governmental rules and regulations. The procedures and norms that the agency has developed over the years and with which it feels most comfortable can be taken "off the shelf" and applied to each new project. Donors often suggest that the failure to move to program aid is related to legitimate concerns about the ability of governments to manage the aid resources appropriately. What is striking, however, is how little donors have moved to program aid, even in countries that have demonstrated a great deal of commitment to making aid more effective and to policy and governance probity. Thus, it makes some sense to limit the degree of program aid in a country like Togo, but it is striking how little more program aid Ghana gets than its corrupt neighbor and how slowly the donors have moved to the new modalities. My argument here is that the primary constraint on the reform of aid modalities is the comfort level of the aid bureaucracies.

An excellent example of these dynamics can be found in the organization of the Consultative Group meetings, in which a recipient government meets with its primary donors to discuss debt and aid issues. A recent World Bank study noted that the overwhelming majority of Consultative Group meetings, the biggest forum for donor and government coordination over aid and government policy, continued to be held outside the borrowing country—typically in Paris or Washington. Of 209 meetings between 1992 and 1999, only 16—or 8 percent—were held in the borrowing country (World Bank 2001b, 13). The Bank report notes that one of the perceived advantages of not holding it in the capital of the borrowing country was the greater likelihood that more senior donor staff would attend a meeting in Paris or Washington. The report does not discuss whether the inconvenience of holding the meeting outside the recipient country dissuaded government officials from attending.

External Accountability

A major problem is that the present mechanisms for accountability of donor organizations to either their own governments or recipient governments do not address the reform issues discussed in this book. In fact, each bilateral aid agency has a distinctive relationship with its government. While some European agencies appear to have a great deal of autonomy, an agency like USAID has been consistently undermined by the micromanagement of its congressional overseers (Lancaster 2000). Oversight only rarely contributes to greater aid effectiveness along the lines advocated in this book. Congressional earmarking of USAID funds is less reprehensible, but it inhibits the agency's flexibility and responsiveness to recipient government objectives and thus undermines government ownership.

More to the point, donor governments have rarely pressured their aid agencies to promote the kinds of reform that have been discussed in this book. On the contrary, existing accountability mechanisms often tend to reinforce the status quo. In the United States, auditing, program evaluation, and the new "results-oriented" approach have actually prevented USAID from experimenting with promising new programming modalities, such as the PRSP. Because agencies are under pressure to show concrete, positive results from their interventions, they are more likely to promote standalone projects, in which achievements can be directly linked to the inputs and activities undertaken under the project with the agency's resources.

External Domestic Pressures on Donors

It is well known that aid agencies face specific domestic pressures that militate against more effective aid. Persistently unhelpful donor practices are linked to domestic pressures that donors cannot avoid. One long-standing example of this is related to aid-tying practices of bilateral donors, where donor agency procurement of goods and services is limited to domestic companies and personnel. Aid tying has long been criticized in the aid effectiveness literature (Jepma 1991, 1994). Because it lessens market competition, it lowers the value of aid to the recipient—by an estimated 15 to 30 percent. In addition, it increases managerial costs to the recipient-country government, which has to deal with equipment purchased from a large number of countries and is unable to integrate and coordinate donor-financed procurement with its own. Finally, it undermines government ownership of aid, since the government does not control procurement and hiring procedures. Yet, domestic interests have put pressure on governments to maintain these practices, which have not been significantly reduced over the last couple of decades despite several attempts to have them circumscribed ("Gifts with Strings Attached," *The Economist,* June 17, 2000; "Brussels Moved to Untie Aid—With a Caveat," *The Guardian*, November 19, 2002).

Less well understood, perhaps, is the extent to which even domestic supporters of aid in the Western democracies do not necessarily promote the kinds of reforms that the aid system needs today. The major impediment to reform of the aid system is the absence of a clear constituency for change within the donor countries and within aid recipients. The general public in the West supports (and sometimes opposes) aid, based on a rather romantic and vague idea of how it works. Thus the public may be for or against budgetary allocations for aid, but it cannot constitute a force for aid agency accountability because it lacks adequate knowledge of how the system works.

Aid's real constituency in the West are the groups that live off aid resources: beneficiaries of procurement, consulting firms, NGOs, academics, grantees, and so on. However well intentioned, these groups have little real incentive to change the way the system now works. Some of these constituencies, notably the Western NGOs, have used their growing clout to push an agenda of change within the aid agencies, but they have focused virtually all their efforts on promoting new issues, such as the environment or governance (Wade 2001, Fox and Brown 1998). Their views of aid modalities and management are actually extremely traditional (Reusse 2002). Indeed, Western NGOs have an interest in the continuation of independent project-type assistance, since they have been playing an increasing role in the implementation of project aid. However sincere in their desire to promote more effective aid, NGOs and their staff are structured to undertake project assistance and be independent of the recipient-state structures.

What to Do?

Foreign aid has been the primary instrument with which the international community has sought to jump-start the economies of the stagnant low-income states (SLIS). Although it is recognized that a successful economic strategy will require the full harnessing of the private sector, these economies are currently unable to attract significant private investment and generally unable to benefit much from the international trading system. For the foreseeable future, their main link to the global economy is foreign aid. Yet aid has been least effective in the stagnant low-income states. Doubts about its effectiveness have led to a wave of aid reform in the last decade. The previous chapters argued that two facts have undermined the impact of sometimes quite promising donor reforms. First, external pressures on and dynamics within donor organizations lead them to fail to fully implement these well-intentioned reforms. As a result, many of the key issues, such as donor coordination, have never been properly addressed. Second, specific governance characteristics in the stagnant low-income states continue to undermine the effectiveness of foreign aid.

The biggest difficulty is not that the policy analyst does not know what to do. The previous chapters suggest a number of desirable reforms. The real difficulty is finding the political and institutional actors who will fully implement these reforms because it is in their interest to do so. A central argument of this book is that the last two decades suggest that the absence of a constituency for reform has been the primary constraint on positive change in the stagnant low-income states.

How should one think of an approach to positive change in stagnant low-income states? The World Bank's Low Income Countries Under Stress

(LICUS) group recently attempted to put together a strategy (LICUS Task Force 2002). The group focused on a slightly different and more varied set of countries than the ones addressed in this book. LICUS includes countries in civil war, for instance, as well as those recovering from civil war. But LICUS is an attempt to put together a strategy and thus worth examining. LICUS starts with much the same diagnostic about its categorization of low-income states as that made in this book. If anything, the LICUS group's understanding of the governance deficiencies of these countries is even more negative than the understanding in this book, since LICUS includes states that have entirely collapsed. The LICUS prescription for these countries is simple: Donors should focus on delivering services to populations and develop pragmatic institutional solutions for doing so. The LICUS report (LICUS Task Force 2002) recognizes that in the long run, it is desirable to have strong and effective state institutions spearheading the development process; but in the short run, these states are weak and thus donors should create and rely on "independent service authorities" (ISAs) to provide developmental goods and services to populations. The report adds that donors should simultaneously work on developing state capacity so that the ISAs can eventually be turned over to the state. Nonetheless, the LICUS approach is to promote economic growth first, with the assumption that governance deficiencies will be easier to address in the future, once growth has resumed.

LICUS is refreshingly forthright and pragmatic. Clearly, recipient-government weakness is the central conundrum of aid to low-income countries. But how is the LICUS strategy different from what donors have always done? For the last 40 years, donors have sidestepped the state with their own aid-driven institutions for short-term practical reasons and simultaneously sought to build capacity within the state, often at great expense. The report is usefully candid about the problems of implementing aid in these countries, but its advocacy of ISAs appears to ignore the many evaluations that have for many years pointed to the ISAs' relatively high cost, mediocre performance, and poor records of sustainability (e.g., see Cassen et al. [1986] for evidence). Although LICUS voices all of the right concerns for ownership and selectivity, it is terribly vague about how the Bank will avoid the past pitfalls in this strategy's implementation. The fact that it advances the use of ISAs as an original and novel approach does not inspire confidence.

The diagnostic offered by LICUS (and this book) does point to the key issue: How can outsiders promote development in countries with governments not particularly interested in development? To answer this question, several broad principles have to be part of any reform strategy:

Create the right incentives. It seems axiomatic to me that reforms that require exceptional leadership, or that do not take into account the incentives individuals and organizations face, are unlikely to succeed. It is true that there is no real substitute for visionary leadership, so that a small number of poor economies will emerge because of great leaders, despite various structural constraints and the dysfunctional relationships described in the book. More prosaically, in a small number of cases, selflessly dedicated public officials, foreign experts, or NGO leaders can advance development and poverty reduction against great odds. But obviously such individuals are a rare luxury, and policies that require exceptional individuals to succeed will fail most of the time. Instead, reform should promote institutions that create incentives to improve the behavior of individuals in both donor organizations and recipient countries, even when these individuals are not exceptional. This may seem obvious, but a striking number of proposed reforms advanced in the development business appear to count on extraordinary individual behavior.

Conditionality and selectivity are both necessary but for different purposes. Any solution will necessarily involve some form of external conditionality by donors. Giving a blank check to all low-income governments with systematic governance problems is almost inevitably likely to prove counterproductive, as indeed the recent past has demonstrated. Even if it is true that traditional forms of conditionality are probably inappropriate in countries that have demonstrated their ability to effectively manage their economic affairs, the stagnant low-income states require an external push, given their governance deficiencies.

Conditionality came under much fire in the 1990s and was pronounced a failure by an odd combination of NGO and academic critics who viewed its application as excessively harsh (e.g., Cornia, Jolly, and Stewart 1987) and by development-community insiders who viewed its application as excessively lenient (e.g., Collier 1997, Killick 1998). I argue that conditionality has often been applied in a flawed manner: It has undermined local ownership over economic policymaking and has proved difficult to reconcile with need-based allocation of aid. Nonetheless, some form of performance-based allocation of aid resources is a sine qua non of reform. The past two decades show clearly that poorly performing states are more likely to pursue policies that are unfavorable to economic development if they know donors will nonetheless continue to provide them with the same level of resources. Carefully implemented donor conditionality is useful because it provides incentives to governments to change their behavior, and it strengthens the hand of reformers within these countries.

How can donors reconcile performance-based allocation of aid with other considerations? I argue that both selectivity and conditionality should be applied to aid. On the one hand, donors should strictly enforce a simple and highly explicit form of selectivity in the political realm as well as over a small number of macroeconomic criteria. On the other hand, donors should engage in a policy dialogue with governments in most areas of sectoral policy using more traditional forms of project conditionality.

No reform can succeed without donor coordination. Any reform program has to have the broad adherence of all the major donors. Any policy not adopted by a majority of the big donors will be ineffective, because the actions of other donors will serve to undermine that policy and send ambiguous signals, at best, to recipient governments. Unless a majority of donors are coordinating their conditionality, one donor's bilateral conditionality is likely to be little more than a passing annoyance to a recipient country that receives hundreds of millions of dollars from two dozen donors. Thus, donor coordination is essential to any successful reform program. It might be added that this coordination increasingly has to take into account the views and actions of leading NGOs, since their lack of adherence to a consensus among official donors will dilute conditionality and the incentives for reform.

In many donor discussions, the need for donor coordination is viewed as justifying a greater resort to "common pool" financing, where donors put their funds into a common pool of resources, which is then available to the government for its developmental activities (Kanbur, Sandler, and Morrison 1999). The World Bank's Poverty Reduction Strategy Papers (PRSP) approach is designed with a common pool logic. I agree that such an approach is long overdue in well-performing countries that have effective governments with a long-term development strategy and the public administration to carry it out. In those countries, uncoordinated, project-driven assistance is unnecessarily obtrusive and inefficient. However, in the stagnant low-income states, where poor performance is in large part due to governance problems, a common pool approach amounts to giving the government a blank check and will not promote development. I agree that even the least effective governments need to be given more responsibilities in the managing of aid resources. I highlight later several such mechanisms that serve to build government ownership and institutional capacity. However, I do not believe the goal of building government ownership and institutional capacity implies the implementation of common pool approaches. Instead, donor agencies should promote coordination with limited pooling of resources, resorting more often to a "lead donor" model in which one donor is designated for a sector and put in charge of the policy dialogue with the government. Similarly, donors need to promote coordination mechanisms to limit the number of projects and donors present in any single country.

Institutional improvements require economic stability and vice versa. The biggest challenge in the stagnant low-income states is that it is equally hard to imagine economic growth without prior improvements in the institutional landscape and improvements in institutional capacity without a prior period of sustained macroeconomic stability. First, it is hard to imagine progress on enhancing institutional capacity without macro-economic stability, since economic crisis causes or exacerbates many of the problems associated with low capacity. The erosion of real civil ser-vice salaries in countries under more or less permanent fiscal crisis has been devastating for state capacity and has encouraged rent-seeking and corruption that now militate against successful economic reform (van de Walle 2001). In periods of extended economic crisis, economic agents shorten their time horizon in their investment decisions, whereas the kinds of organizational and economic investments needed most for growth re-quire relatively long-term decisions. Institution building probably requires a stable macroeconomy, with minimum uncertainty. Similarly, govern-ment ownership of the development process is much less likely if recipient governments are engaged in the kind of crisis management that has ex-isted in most low-income states over the last 20 years. Second, the last several decades at the same time suggest that institutional constraints have hampered macroeconomic stability and sustainable growth in the stagnant low-income states. Political instability, predatory state officials, and a haphazard regulatory environment all undermine private invest-ment. Nondevelopmental state structures driven by clientelism are likely to face endemic fiscal imbalances.

Faced with such a classic chicken-or-egg question, should reformers focus on institutions or on economic stability first? Moreover, what should donors do that they are not already doing in the stagnant low-income states? After all, the last few years have already witnessed a growing focus on governance issues, in addition to the last two decades' focus on macroeconomic stabilization. These questions do not have easy an-swers. A renewed attention to both economic growth and central-state capacity issues does seem desirable. Again, the contrast with the LICUS approach and its twin focus on social-service delivery by nonstate actors should be clear. So should the donors' recent emphasis on promoting local government and NGOs as alternatives to the central state.

From experience, one knows there are no magic bullets to getting the SLIS economies back on track. In the following paragraphs, I discuss a number of approaches that will help promote the change these countries need to benefit from economic growth and the role that the Western donors could play in advancing these changes. Nonetheless, these coun-tries have highly problematic structural features and historical legacies, and it bears repeating that positive change will not be easy to engineer. As argued in the previous chapter, reform of the aid business has typi-cally been stalled because of the absence of a powerful constituency for change in both the West and the developing world. Aid reform is likely to be least tractable in the stagnant low-income states. Some clearly desir-able reforms may be impossible to implement, for a combination of politi-cal and capacity reasons. Progress is likely to be slow and discontinuous, and the solutions offered here will not be without their own contradictions and problems.

Promote Democracy in the Stagnant Low-Income States

Democracy is no panacea, *yet liberal political reform that increases political participation and competition has to be part of the equation that brings economic growth and poverty alleviation to these countries.* This is true, first, because the balance of empirical evidence suggests that democracies outperform nondemocracies; for a long time, economists posited a "cruel choice" between democracy and growth, arguing that political participation prevented governments from deferring consumption in favor of the long-term investments that spur growth (Przeworski, Stokes, and Manin 1999). A new round of empirical studies in the last decade has, however, not upheld the authoritarian advantage hypothesis, concluding instead that there is probably a small but significant "democratic advantage" (for an excellent literature review, see Gerring, Barndt, and Bond [2003]).

Second, as argued earlier, the poor economic performance of the stagnant low-income states is hard to disassociate from their authoritarian politics. Even if some authoritarian countries have managed to engineer significant economic growth, this is clearly not the case for these states, where the political status quo seems dysfunctional from an economic point of view. In particular, the political patterns I identified as "presidentialism" appear to be inimical to growth.

In fact, recent World Bank–sponsored research (Kaufmann 2003) suggests that governance improvements can have a positive impact on the level of economic growth. As suggested earlier, the traditional donor approach—most recently embodied by LICUS—suggests a causal mechanism that goes from growth to governance, so that donors can ignore governance issues, which will tend to improve over time as the local economy gets richer. This research suggests the opposite: The causal arrow goes from governance to growth, and a higher income level will have much less of an impact on governance than the reverse.

Donors continue to be ambivalent about making their aid programs compatible with national-level democracy. Economists and engineers have dominated the donor community, and perhaps as a result it has paid closer attention to economic policy and technical issues and inadequate attention to institutional issues. For many years, donors clung to the argument that aid allocation should not take into account the political orientation of the recipient country, because it was irrelevant to the donors' work. That donors should not interfere in the domestic politics of recipient countries remains a deeply entrenched norm in many aid agencies. In fact, external support for a government is necessarily a profoundly political act, since it provides resources to the incumbent that the political opposition does not receive. In addition, even on the donors' narrow technical terms, aid and politics are connected, since a number of studies have demonstrated that political factors have an effect on the ability of aid to promote development (e.g., Svensson 1999). Indeed, World Bank research in the 1990s (Isham, Kaufmann, and Pritchett 1997) makes clear that the level of political and civil rights in a country actually has had an effect on the rate of return of World Bank projects there. Even so, the Bank has only recently begun to involve itself in governance issues and continues to define them in the relatively narrow context of economic management.

To be sure, economic policy orientation is also important, and economic growth almost certainly cannot be engineered in these countries without the prior success of macroeconomic stabilization. Investors will not return until they are certain that the macro climate is healthy in a sustainable way after years of fiscal and monetary imbalances. Similarly, technical issues are also important. Some irrigation pumps really are better than others; scarce resources can be saved and productivity enhanced if certain technical choices are made rather than others. Having said that, the earlier analysis should have made it clear that governance deficiencies are a key economic constraint in stagnant low-income states.

Why would democratization help bring about economic growth and poverty alleviation in the stagnant low-income states? Presidentialism concentrates power in the executive and shields it from accountability. As discussed earlier, long-standing "strongmen" presidents who are virtually above the law tend to characterize the stagnant low-income states. Prebendal forms of clientelism are used to promote political stability, but they subvert formal political institutions, generate substantial inequalities, and undermine private-sector growth. The key benefit of democratization is that it engenders the vertical and horizontal accountability that is necessary to discipline the executive branch of government. Some will argue that donors have already assimilated this lesson and are using political conditionality to improve governance in developing countries. As argued earlier, however, the donors have been neither consistent nor persistent in their application of conditionality. In particular, the absence of donor coordination on political conditionality has served to diffuse the collective signal donors send to low-income governments. One donor's tough conditionality will have little impact if other donors have not followed suit. Cutting total aid by 50 percent to a country will not necessarily change a government's behavior if it still receives the equivalent of 10 percent of GDP in aid, or if the government is justified to believe that the larger aid volume will resume in 12 to 18 months, regardless of its behavior. As a result, it is important to realize that successful political conditionality will require much greater coordination than has been realized in the past.

Political selectivity should send a clear signal to governments that certain behaviors will no longer be tolerated. While all forms of clientelism cannot realistically be eliminated, the worst kinds of governance break-downs can and should be sanctioned systematically. Ideally, donors should in the short-to-medium term work to eliminate prebendal forms of clientelism and to circumscribe patronage to more reasonable levels in the medium-to-long term, since the former undermines economic growth much more than the latter.

Donors complain that they are poorly equipped to make precise judgments about the domestic governance of recipient countries. Certain regimes are nonetheless easy to evaluate. For instance, a small number of states still have military governments in power that came to power through the barrel of a gun or that do not hold regular elections. I believe these are easy calls: *Military governments should not receive a penny of donor assistance*, and a sharply reduced volume of aid should be directed to non-governmental actors, until the military return to the barracks and an elected government is formed. Cutting off these countries would send a clear message that old-fashioned authoritarian forms of government are no longer acceptable. They should certainly not receive loans from the international financial institutions (IFIs), as the recent past suggests this will inexorably turn into odious debt and saddle future generations with unfair obligations.

Such cases are few. Among the stagnant low-income states, only two governments could be defined as traditional military governments at the time of writing (Pakistan and the Central African Republic), though the military was playing a preponderant role in the politics of three others (Comoros, the Gambia, and Guinea-Bissau), and several others had long traditions of military involvement in politics. Comoros, for instance, has suffered through 19 coups since independence in 1975. Particularly today, authoritarian leaders have realized that they can get away with various rather superficial concessions to democratic governance that do not threaten their rule, such as regular elections they do not lose or the allowing of parliamentary oppositions that are never allowed to win more than a small minority of seats.

Most donors resist political conditionality or selectivity in a number of ways. First, they argue there is a real risk that the cutting off of aid will enhance political instability. As the World Bank's LICUS Task Force puts it, "Countries abandoned by the international development community show few signs of autonomous recovery . . . such countries are also at risk of state failure" (LICUS Task Force 2002, iv). To be sure, such a risk exists, but one would be hard-pressed to come up with many examples in which the termination of aid can be causally linked to the emergence of state collapse. Indeed, many countries that have undergone state collapse enjoyed a large amount of aid right before they collapsed. Donors provided Rwanda some $356 million in aid in 1993, the year before the genocide, equivalent to $47 per capita. Liberia, Sierra Leone, and Somalia received $28, $25, and $69 in aid per capita, respectively, in their last year of relative societal stability before state collapse. Even if one does not agree with Peter Uvin's (1998) harsh verdict that the aid system was in part to blame for state collapse in a country like Rwanda, it seems clear that large amounts of aid did not anticipate or prevent state collapse.

Second, donors resist political conditionality or selectivity by arguing that it is very difficult to make judgments about exactly how competitive and participatory formally democratic national processes are. Even here, however, the donors can use telltale signs to evaluate the true nature of governance. The absence of alternation in power is one clear sign. Leaders who have been in power for several decades are not presiding over democratic systems. As a result, I believe *donors should withdraw from countries in which the constitution does not provide for term limits or in which the leader has been in power for longer than, say, 12 years,* which would amount to three four-year presidential terms. In fact the 12-year cut-off point works extremely well. In 7 of the 9 stagnant low-income states evaluated as "not free" by Freedom House at the end of 2003 (see table 2.2), leaders have been in power more than 12 years.[1] A perceptive reader of an earlier draft of this book pointed out, however, that Seewoosagur Ramgoolam was prime minister of Mauritius from 1968 to 1982, while Seretse Khama was president of Botswana between independence in 1966 and his death in 1980. Would I recommend the termination of aid to these leaders, who in retrospect were exemplary developers? Clearly, these would have been tough cases to cut off, and perhaps both countries might have benefited from an exception. On the other hand, I suspect neither country's economic performance would have suffered all that much if either leader had left power a couple years earlier. In fact, in both cases, it was the democratic alternation of power at the end of the first leader's rule after independence that confirmed the regime's governance qualities.

Donors also often resist pulling out of authoritarian countries, arguing that the recipient regime has begun a process of positive political reform, so external pressure would be counterproductive at best. Sure enough, in cases such as Ghana in the 1990s, an authoritarian government was able to undertake a phased process of political liberalization. Eliminating aid to former president Jerry Rawlings' government in the mid-1990s might very well have been counterproductive in terms of advancing political liberalization. But the donors have much more commonly erred in the other direction—of justifying the continuation of assistance to authoritarian rulers on the basis of vague promises of political reform. There are no doubt situations in which it is wiser to put discrete pressure on governments to change certain manifestations of poor governance and in which a withdrawal of aid can have negative consequences. However,

---

1. The exceptions are President Pervez Musharraf of Pakistan and President François Bozizé of the Central African Republic.

my main point here is that clear and explicit governance "triggers" for cutting off aid can be applied in a way that sends a clear signal to recipients.

A similar objection to the establishment of explicit rules cutting off nondemocratic countries from aid comes from a geostrategic perspective: Key allies need to be propped up, regardless of how distasteful the regime in place is. At the present time, such an argument is made for Pakistan, for instance, viewed as a key ally in the struggle against terrorism. True, the current regime in Pakistan is highly imperfect but is probably preferable to the likely alternative if it should fall and assists us in reaching various other objectives. There are two responses to this argument. First, propping up a dictator who does not enjoy domestic support is at best a very temporary solution, and if maintained for more than a very brief period, is almost always a self-fulfilling prophecy. For instance, three decades of generous Western support to Zaire did help to maintain in power an incompetent and extraordinarily venal government that enjoyed little support, but the aid did not prevent that country from collapse and warlord rule in the mid-1990s. Surely, one of the lessons of the last half-century is that it is naive and false to think that large amounts of aid will assist a process of governance reform in poorly governed countries. Assistance is far more likely to allow bad governments to remain bad.

In addition, if geostrategic pressures compel governments to assist unsavory regimes, it is very important that the assistance not involve traditional aid agencies. Governments balance different foreign policy objectives; insofar as possible, aid agencies should focus on only one objective —the development of the recipient countries. Donor agencies that adopt other objectives as their own, such as their governments' security or commercial aims or both, are bound to lose both credibility and effectiveness as purveyors of development assistance. Instead, governments should use other agencies to provide assistance to advance security or commercial objectives. This would help make it clear to recipients that the donors were not exercising conditionality inconsistently.

Build a New Aid Relationship

The current relationship between donors and the stagnant low-income states does not promote the right kinds of incentives to low-income governments to use aid well and promote economic development, though some undoubtedly do so. Donor micromanagement of aid undermines local ownership, while the large volume of aid that donors give still does not take enough account of developmental performance, failing either to reward governments committed to good policies and sound governance or to withdraw or reduce aid to poorly performing states. The following discussion seeks to change this in order to improve incentives for governments face to promote development.

Accept the Possibility of Lower Volumes of Official Development Assistance

Conditionality is not credible if donors are not willing to accept the possibility that aid volume will decline in specific countries, at least in the short-to-medium term. The selectivity model is right to argue that donors have to change the incentives for recipient governments. This means that fundamentally, donors have to find ways to clearly and unambiguously reward governments that are doing the right thing. Few observers in the aid community are willing to make explicit one virtually inevitable consequence of this critical principle: that aid volume to certain countries is likely to decline in the first phase of a real selectivity strategy. Yet it is probably the bureaucratic attachment to a given volume of aid being fixed ahead of time that is the biggest obstacle to the implementation of a real selectivity strategy.

Make no mistake, cutting off aid entirely is a harsh medicine, particularly in countries with high levels of poverty. But it is necessary, given the four decades of mixed messages that donors have given recipient governments. Having failed so miserably to enforce conditionality for so long, donors now have little choice but to implement unforgiving conditionality if they are to gain back credibility and leverage. The data presented earlier suggest that aid has become at best slightly more selective in recent years. Yet, to change the incentives for recipient governments, the allocation of aid needs to be unambiguously selective.

I am not necessarily advocating a decline in overall aid volume. If the application of conditionality does imply a sharp reduction in aid to certain low-income economies, it should also lead to increases in the flow of resources to well-performing countries, either in the form of aid or in the form of quicker and more generous debt relief. In addition, the donors could devote a larger share of resources to regional programs and for the provision of global public goods: They remain woefully underfunded, and their success does not require the developmental commitment of individual low-income governments.

Conditionality strategies have in many instances been undermined by the difficulties in calibrating the volume of aid that should go to countries that meet some but not all of the conditions. In practice, donors will often let governments slide and maintain the aid program despite governments' failure to meet some of the conditions because donors are hesitant to punish governments that are meeting most of the conditions. On the other hand, this leads donors to finally withdraw their aid from governments for relatively anodyne reasons, when a number of minor failures to comply have added up over time. Monitoring compliance is not easy and imposes judgments over which reasonable people will disagree. But it seems better than the system with which the European Union is experimenting, notably in Uganda (Adam and Gunning 2002), where it calibrates its aid precisely to the number of conditions the government meets. In such a system, if the government complies with two-thirds of the conditions, it gets two-thirds of the aid. Such a system requires even more donor monitoring and appears to lead to the worst kind of donor micromanagement. Indeed, in the current situation, good performers that have a good track record of complying with the most important conditions tend to get more detailed conditionality over clearly secondary issues that involve more donor involvement rather than less in day-to-day policymaking. On the other hand, the bad performers get somewhat less money but also get more leeway on secondary issues, which makes little sense.

My view is that a small number of clear conditions with unambiguous measurement criteria can be applied as part of a selectivity strategy. These should focus on the governance criteria outlined earlier and on basic macroeconomic policy issues, such as the size of the fiscal deficit or the basic parameters of monetary policy. Sectoral policy issues or, say, the pace of privatization should perhaps be the topic of policy dialogue with recipient governments in the context of traditional, project-level conditionality but should not be the subject of formal conditionality. Thus, for instance, the failure of a government to undertake price liberalization as promised might lead to the freezing of a big agricultural project but should not affect other donor lending. Instead, there should be only a small number of obvious conditions that could trigger a wholesale withdrawal, known to the public in the recipient countries, so that noncompliance is not controversial, does not require interference or donor micromanagement, and the incentives to comply are not ambiguous.

In addition, this new mixture of selectivity and traditional conditionality should be accompanied by other reforms of the way in which aid is carried out, outlined in the following paragraphs.

Adopt the Foundation Model

The only way to promote local ownership of the development process and to reward states that are committed to development is to adopt what has come to be known as the "foundation model," though in fairness it does not appear that many foundations actually work in this manner. In this approach, the donor agency waits until the recipient government makes a proposal for support, and the agency does not have a set target for the volume of aid it wants to extend to any country. It also may establish broad, general priorities for its aid, but the extent and nature of each individual country program are entirely determined by the quality of the proposals that the agency receives.

Current efforts to promote local ownership fall well short. As discussed earlier, policies to promote stakeholder participation remain micromanaged by donors and undermined by *ventriloquism*, in which governments are made to understand what policies they need to adopt in order to receive donor support, often with the assistance of long-term foreign experts provided by the same donors. Regardless of the rhetoric of local empowerment and participation, the current PRSP programs remains identifiably donor programs, with tangential relations to the governmental budget process, weak local constituencies, and a large-scale and costly donor presence to manage the process.

In the foundation model, the donors wait relatively passively until governments or other local actors come to them with proposals. The burden of coming up with good proposals is up to the governments. Clearly, there are dangers to the foundation model, and it is not a panacea. It, too, favors the governments that least need aid, since they are more likely to have the wherewithal to make reasonable proposals that donors will find acceptable. Governments that do not value development, which is surely the case for some of the 26 stagnant low-income states, will generate fewer proposals. Perhaps, though this would have the advantage of dispelling any doubts donors can have about the absence of ownership in these countries. Governments in these countries would then be penalized for their absence of commitment to development and not continue to be spoon fed official development assistance (ODA). Moreover, donors could still accept project proposals from nongovernmental sources in the country.

Perhaps more problematically, it could be predicted that recipient governments would simply make the proposals they believe the donor wants to hear, leading to a new form of ventriloquism. Even relatively capacity-weak governments could employ intermediaries to generate proposals to gain funding for activities the government had little intention of carrying out. This would clearly be a danger, but the burden of having to put a proposal together and thus acquiring the capacity to do so would presumably partly integrate aid projects and programs into government decision making; the donors' evaluation of the proposals could emphasize issues such as local stakeholder participation and sustainability, which today too often get little attention.

This means eliminating donor-driven initiatives, of which the PRSP process is merely the latest in a long series. There is no reason the government's own budgetary and planning process cannot serve as the sole framework within which donors provide their aid. Such an approach would result in significant savings; the current system relies on high levels of investment in external monitoring and evaluation services to attempt to overcome the pervasive principal-agent hazards posed by aid's externally driven approach.

Promote Greater Donor Transparency

Experts in public management agree that bureaucracies that are not accountable to the publics they serve are less likely to perform well than those that are. The more bureaucracies are shielded from their clients, the more their behavior will be dictated by internal bureaucratic concerns that may be quite at odds with their official objectives. This kind of goal displacement is common in bureaucracies, and the literature has identified a number of cures, including greater transparency in bureaucratic decision making and increased competition across organizations.

Donor organizations have been increasingly willing to apply these lessons to the developing-country bureaucracies they have been seeking to reform. But aid bureaucracies have been largely unwilling to apply the same lessons to their own operations. Transparency has improved in recent years but rarely vis-à-vis the public in developing countries. Under political pressures, donors have opened up their books and, to a lesser extent, their internal decision making to Western NGOs operating in Western capitals or to their own national parliaments (Lancaster 2000). On the other hand, much less information is available to the public of recipient countries. Recipient governments, for their part, have accepted this situation, which typically conforms to their own lack of transparency and allows them to escape accountability to their own publics.

At the individual country level, there is little transparency concerning the details of donor projects, from the beneficiaries of grants to procurement decisions and hiring procedures. This needs to change in order to promote greater accountability for the donors vis-à-vis their primary clients, the citizens of the countries they assist. A detailed accounting of aid expenditures at the local level is long overdue; it would promote the accountability of aid agencies and of the organizations and activities they finance in these countries. The information provided to citizens would also facilitate public debates about the opportunity costs of different aid activities, a debate that is currently absent.

Strengthen the DAC

The Organization for Economic Cooperation and Development's (OECD) Development Assistance Committee (DAC) should be reinforced and made more independent of donor agencies. At present, it is too often a cozy club of retired and delegated bilateral aid agency officials, who compliment each other on the fine job their respective governments are doing in the aid field. Yet, it is a long-standing institution that has gained valuable experience in information sharing and data collection at the level of the donors. With greater independence and a mandate for constructive criticism of the donors, it could play a much more useful role than it does today as the official cheerleader of the aid business. It could, for instance, promote donor coordination and greater consistency in donor procedures in areas such as auditing and procurement, where donor differences impose a substantial managerial burden on recipient governments.

Build State Capacity

A cornerstone of a new approach must be to create incentives for governments to increase their institutional capacity. Throughout this book, I have emphasized the importance of a greater focus on institutional capacity, and I have argued that donors need to get away from the projectization of capacity building, to see it as an end in itself rather than something that is done in the context of an aid project with other objectives.

Adopt the "Local" Model

The elements of the foundation model recommended earlier should be complemented by what Tom Carothers has called "localism," based on his work with the Soros Foundations in Eastern Europe (Carothers 1996). This form of aid programming relies much more systematically on local capacities for developmental expertise in two distinct but complementary ways. First, the approach views the objective of aid not as the promotion of abstract objectives such as "economic growth," "institution building," or "democracy promotion" but as supporting and advancing the individuals and civic associations that are most likely to foster some local variant of these objectives. In Eastern Europe, Carothers argues that the Soros Foundations have been very successful at supporting a large number of individuals and small organizations with small grants to allow them to carry out activities that will advance democracy and capitalism in the long run.

This approach has the advantage of increasing the local demand for a more effective central state, since the historical experience suggests that a rich and vibrant civil society stimulates a more responsive and effective state apparatus (Putnam 1992). Carothers' analysis does suggest it will work best in countries such as those of Eastern Europe, where the central state has relatively high capacity. On the other hand, a purely local approach may prove problematic in countries with extremely weak state capacity, which is true of most of the stagnant low-income states. Small associations may be extremely useful for the provision of critical social services, complementing the state in cost-effective ways. They may be necessary to pressure the state into better behavior by forcing accountability and undermining public monopolies. But they cannot replace the state, because they are much less useful for the provision of public goods and basic infrastructure. Thus, following the local approach does not obviate the need to undertake a complementary direct effort at central-state institutional development.

Second, the local approach promotes developmental expertise by dramatically cutting down the role of foreign experts and relying instead on local expertise for different facets of the design, implementation, monitoring, and evaluation of aid activities. This has the advantage of being cheap. Despite some progress, the aid business remains overwhelmingly reliant on Western consulting firms, universities, and experts, who implement the vast majority of activities throughout the project cycle. Yet, as Carothers notes, a local NGO will implement a project for a small fraction of the cost of an American or West European consulting firm, which allows the Soros Foundation dollar to go much further: "A three-day conference with a group of visiting foreign experts may cost more than $25,000. The same money could fund the entire operating expenses of a medium-sized local NGO for a year" (Carothers 1996, 21).

But the local approach also has the much more significant advantage of nurturing and developing local expertise in managerial and technical skills, which are important for long-term development. Donor agencies often protest that the local economy lacks professionals and organizations with the needed skill set. Surely, however, such professionals would emerge if a local market existed that increased the overt demand for such expertise, as more professionals would stay in the country rather than drive taxis in Western cities. Initially, the reliance on local actors might result in greater corruption, and no doubt inexperience might generate mistakes. But the emergence of a competitive market for local expertise would eventually help drive out the incompetent and help promote the more professional agents. Moreover, mistakes would be much cheaper than they are at present, given the much lower salaries that would prevail.

A side effect of the current prevalence of foreign experts and consulting firms is that their salary structure pushes up all salaries in the local aid business. Thus, local staff of Western aid agencies and NGOs tend to have extremely high salaries by local standards, thus distorting the local wage scale. Relying much more systematically on local professionals would almost certainly soon bring down local personnel costs within local NGOs and project units, as the demand would generate its own supply. Carothers gives the example of the Soros Foundation office in Romania, in which all the personnel were Romanian. The office had twice as much staff as the USAID office in the country, at least in part because of its more intense and hands-on management practices, but at a fraction of the cost of USAID, largely because the latter hired so many expensive American expatriates (Carothers 1996, 18). The aid business may well be justified in paying slightly higher-than-average wages to attract good local staff, but the current extremely large premiums are driven more by the comparison with the remuneration of foreign experts than anything else.

In sum, the current reliance on foreign expertise needs to be curtailed. In practical terms, it would not be unreasonable to recommend that *donors reduce the use of foreign staff and experts, as well as foreign consulting firms not based in country, by half within the next five years.*

Adopting more of the logic of the local approach would also move the aid business closer to the "capacity utilization" approach that experts of institution building have recently endorsed (Grindle and Hilderbrand 1995; Fukuda-Parr, Lopes, and Malik 2002). They argue that donors should undertake measures to better utilize the capacity that already exists within recipient countries, rather than focusing capacity-building efforts on creating capacity that then tends to be underutilized. Certain elements of the project cycle could easily be "localized." Thus, I recommend that *donors make the evaluation of aid projects and programs a local responsibility.* Again, the comparison with how foundations work is instructive: They demand evaluations from their recipients, who know they must deliver a credible accounting of aid monies if they wish to receive further support from the foundation. It is striking that the vast majority of low-income recipient states currently undertake no evaluation of aid, which is considered a donor task. Indeed, few governments have more than a pro forma role in evaluation exercises, which are typically undertaken by and for the donors, and it is unusual for ministries to make use of donor evaluations for their own sectoral programming activities.

This recipient passivity and donor dominance of evaluation processes are perplexing. First, it would make more sense for the recipient to undertake the evaluation rather than the aid agency for which there is a clear conflict of interest. Local agencies, based in the country, are more likely to have the detailed field knowledge necessary to make a well-informed judgment about the project. Donor agency evaluators, on the other hand, are likely to lack that knowledge and will be under pressure from their employers to make a positive evaluation of their agency colleagues. Indeed, a recurring problem of aid evaluations has been that they tend to exaggerate project benefits and downplay problems. Second, involving more local staff in evaluation would be immensely useful to gaining local ownership of aid programs. Local evaluation would foster a debate about the project and its objectives and generate broader support for successful projects. Clearly, few low-income countries are capable today of taking over the evaluation process; it is nonetheless logical and desirable that efforts be devoted immediately to increase their ability to take over this function in the near future. Governments would, moreover, work to develop this capacity if aid resources depended on it.

Restore Governmental Economic Planning

I have described how aid has tended to favor pseudo state actors such as project units and foreign experts. Such a bias is a mistake, as it both favors the public sector, at the same time emasculating it, and fails to promote a sense of ownership by state agents. More aid can go to private actors than is the case now, as advocated by the local approach just discussed. On the other hand, aid directed to the public sector needs to be better integrated into the work of core state institutions. When resources go to the state, they should be included in national budgets and planning exercises. Parallel donor-driven exercises, whether in the form of the old by-pass model or in the new style of the PRSP, should be eliminated. Instead, all foreign aid should be integrated into national indicative planning exercises as was originally envisioned by the aid system and then progressively abandoned in the 1970s and 1980s. This is hardly a pitch for socialist planning. Instead, it is the recognition that the only way to build real ownership is to encourage governments to take command of their development process through a planning process that results in reasonable economic policies (which was all too rarely the case in the 1960s) and a participatory debate about development choices. I believe that even in the countries with lousy governance records, donors can use economic planning to empower technocrats and build state capacity.

The PRSP process is after all at least in part an attempt to fashion an aid-friendly economic planning structure within low-income governments. Ironically, the World Bank is trying to rebuild planning capacity in low-income countries, having spent much of the 1970s and 1980s trying to close down planning ministries and commissions. Though a step in the right direction, the PRSP is misguided in the sense that the main objective of economic planning should not be to please the donors and qualify for debt relief.

It should be noted that this implies a central role for the state in aid coordination. Much of the current effort to promote coordination is driven by donor concerns and is not compatible with local ownership. Donor attempts to coordinate their own efforts, notably at conditionality, are important, but donor coordination does not have the same function as aid coordination, which is best undertaken by the central state. In the context of a foundation approach, donors might still coordinate their own response to government proposals, but it is important that government aid proposals be integrated into a sustainable and coherent development program, which the government is best suited to develop and sustain.

Take Civil Service Reform Seriously

Perhaps the key institutional actor in the development of state capacity is the civil service. Civil service reform has been a central aspect of the economic recovery of countries like Uganda and Ghana. In such countries, forceful regimes were able to lay off a substantial number of civil servants, provide significant salary increases to remaining employees, and pay them on time, all within a relatively brief period. Not surprisingly, their performance dramatically improved. Yet donors have long underemphasized the civil service in too many countries. In most of the stagnant low-income states, a high degree of politicization over hiring and promotions has weakened if not eliminated the civil service commission. The civil service has been sidelined by the increasing reliance on special implementation structure, often underwritten by the donors. Salary arrears have been allowed to accumulate over more than a decade, adding to the burdens of wage compression, low salaries, and ghost workers.

In sum, even as donors assign a growing number of tasks to these governments, they should provide resources and assistance for a rapid revamping of their civil services.

Beyond Aid

This book has argued that foreign aid will remain the central policy instrument to deal with the stagnant low-income states for the foreseeable future. Nonetheless, the international community can pursue other policies that will help make aid more effective and speed up the development process. Two are worth highlighting in the context of the themes I have explored: more effective promotion of the private sector and a greater attention to regional public institutions.

Promote the Private Sector

A view that has emerged during the last decade is that aid should promote the private sector more effectively. Aid to the stagnant low-income states has often served as a substitute for private capital, bailing out economies with policies that made them unattractive to private investors. Economists have suggested that aid should be designed instead to facilitate private investment. This is now being translated into policies that seek to use aid funds to promote mutually beneficial trade and investment opportunities in low-income states for Western countries through various subsidies to private agents in both sets of countries. This is notably the case with the African trade and investment promotion program—the African Growth and Opportunity Act (AGOA) in Washington in the late 1990s. The logic is impeccable: Aid should help African countries regain their international competitiveness, without which they will remain dependent wards of the donors. Rather than providing aid to governments, why not establish import-export credit facilities, loan guarantee systems, and so on? Such measures in effect subsidize the return of private investors, who otherwise might view the region as too risky, and eventually result in the renewal of growth.

Initiatives to promote the private sector are important. At the same time, the prospects for private-sector growth in these countries are limited. As discussed earlier, the stagnant low-income states have received very little foreign direct investment in recent years. Unfortunately, most of these countries have neither the natural resources nor the internal market to attract investors. The new "trade, not aid" rhetoric is sustained by good old-fashioned commercial motives that, in conjunction with various budgetary pressures and the weakening of the aid impulse, are likely to result in both a smaller and a much less altruistic resource flow. One of the emerging mythologies of proposals such as AGOA is that what is good for Western business will necessarily promote development in the poor countries. In the current political climate, these initiatives may well evolve into boondoggles for the corporate sector of the developed countries and may not be all that different from the tied aid of the past. Moreover, even if well implemented, this approach has little to offer the region's poorer countries, in which the private sector is unlikely to provide the critical investments in poverty alleviation, human capital, and better governance.

The policy community should devote more attention to several other issues, which could promote private sector–led growth more than these schemes to promote Western investment in low-income countries. First, donors tend to focus on "foreign" investment only and to devote much less time to "domestic" investment. Yet, many of the low-income countries have suffered many years of substantial capital flight, and a huge amount of capital now sits in offshore accounts. All investors, foreign and domestic, will respond to similar incentives, but special efforts could be made to discourage capital flight and encourage its repatriation. Banking-sector reform and financial-sector regulation have all been the focus of donor efforts, but the truth is progress has been slow and uncertain. Many stagnant low-income states still lack financial sectors that inspire much confidence, particularly for small local investors who lack political connections.

Second, faster progress on debt relief may well prove as important as investment promotion schemes to revitalize the private sector in the stagnant low-income states. Much evidence suggests that large debt-servicing obligations dampen investment because economic agents see these debts as future obligations for the government that will force it to increase revenue generation in the form of taxation (Birdsall and Williamson 2002, Elbadawi 1996). In addition, governments have less incentive to promote revenue generation when they know that additional revenues will simply return to the donor countries.

Third, Western protectionism in certain sectors of great importance to SLIS economies also needs to be curtailed. The now notorious example of US subsidies for US cotton producers is a great example of this protectionism, since it affects a number of stagnant low-income states. The direct cost of protectionism to low-income countries in the form of forgone exports is relatively high and apparently rising. The indirect cost, in the form of forgone investments by Western investors that are deterred by the possibility of protectionism, may be higher.

Promote Regional Institutions

Western governments need to promote regional organizations, such as the UN economic commissions, regional development banks, and various regional think tanks and research institutes, much more assiduously than they have so far. An advantage of such stronger regional institutions would be a larger role in the promotion of local policy learning and the creation of institutional capacity that would be transmitted to national institutions. Additionally, these institutions could play a role as regional agencies of restraint, establishing regional norms for policy and governance.

Many of the current IFI tasks should be transferred to regional institutions. For instance, these institutions should undertake much of the research currently done by the World Bank and the International Monetary Fund. One immediate advantage would be research of greater immediate concern to the recipient countries themselves. Another would be the development of a cadre of professional policy analysts in the region, which would improve both regional and national policy debates. Today, development research undertaken by the IFIs and the UN system is carried out almost entirely in the West. Indeed, more development research probably occurred in developing-country institutions two decades ago than does today, as economic crisis and structural adjustment resulted in a substantial brain drain from low-income countries (e.g., Eicher 2001). While it may be influential in shaping policy within the IFIs, current research in these international organizations has too little resonance within the developing countries, outside of a handful of individuals in technocratic positions. Since so much of this research appears to support the policy positions of the IFIs in their policy debates with recipient countries, it is in any event often viewed as tainted and not objective by the publics in low-income countries.

Regional organizations could also play a larger role in the form of aid that would promote global public goods (Ferroni and Mody 2002), such as research on tropical diseases and agriculture. These organizations should also promote revamping regional statistical offices to stop the progressive decline in the quality of national economic and social data, which has been observed in the last two decades. In many cases, it makes sense to undertake these activities at the regional level. By all accounts, different global public goods are currently underfunded, given the benefits to be derived from their successful provision. Research on tropical diseases and HIV/AIDS provide good examples. These diseases currently exert an enormous cost on low-income economies, and private-sector investments in devising preventive medicines or improving treatments have been inadequate because of the low purchasing power of the populations most affected. There is little doubt that the social benefits of such investments dwarf the returns to most investments currently made by the aid business. Thus, there is a powerful logic for public intervention at the supranational level.

A Coalition for Change?

From where will the impetus for positive change come? Who will supply the reforms advocated in this book? If my assessment is correct, neither the donor organizations nor the recipient governments can be the main force for change. Internal and external pressures constrain donors, despite the existence of many officials of good will. Recipient governments, despite some well-meaning technocrats, are prey to clientelistic and other nondevelopmental impulses. Unfortunately, this question does not have an easy answer. In rich countries, even when the public supports foreign aid, it typically has an extremely traditional view of aid, with the dominant image being the dedicated Western expert, knee-deep in the rice paddies, implementing a technical assistance project. In all likelihood, the general public views the types of issues discussed in this book as "inside baseball," much too arcane and probably of secondary importance to the success of aid. A sympathetic public (and not all Western publics are all that sympathetic to aid) may be educated to understand the need to lessen the amount of tied aid, for example, or it can be convinced of the need for conditionality, but it is less likely to soon understand the cost of donor proliferation or the relative advantages of moving to programmatic aid. For these reasons, I do not believe that the general public in the West will be part of the aid reform coalition that is needed to promote the views advocated in this book.

One important potential member of a coalition for change can be found in the Western NGO community. Their relatively recent rise to prominence has demonstrated their impressive potential to promote change. They have managed to significantly influence the policy agenda of the official donors in certain policy areas, such as the environment and poverty reduction. Their pressure in the 1990s led to a dilution of donor conditionality in the poorest countries and to greater debt relief. Yet, they have focused almost all their attention on substantive issues and have largely ignored procedural issues and aid modalities. Most have also exerted much more pressure on Western governments than they have on recipient governments. Neither of these biases is inevitable. NGOs have always had a predilection for project-based aid, and the dominant values in the NGO community perhaps make them insensitive to the problems of donor proliferation. Nonetheless, NGOs that care deeply about aid could become more vocal about the need to change aid modalities as discussed in this book. There is no reason NGOs could not more effectively push donors to promote more meaningful donor coordination, for example. Similarly, the NGO community needs to become much more vocal about the governance failures of recipient governments.

The private sector has a long-term interest in promoting positive change as well, since improving the conditions for economic growth would benefit them directly. Businesses will benefit in the long run from improved governance, even if they tend to be suspicious regarding new rules about transparency and accountability. Current proposals to convince private companies to promote revenue transparency for their operations in developing countries, as a way to limit corruption, provide a promising start.

Finally, and most important, the public in the stagnant low-income states also needs to be part of this coalition for change. They have the greatest stake in more effective aid, since it would promote economic development and more effective and democratic governments in the low-income countries. There is a "looking a gift horse in the mouth" dilemma here, perhaps a reason why intellectuals in low-income countries have hesitated to criticize foreign aid in the past. But low-income country publics should become more vocal both to donors and to their governments to improve their performance and stop squandering aid resources.

In this respect, the emergence of more participatory and competitive politics in the stagnant low-income states is extremely encouraging. However imperfect, political liberalization has allowed the emergence of a lively press, various civic organizations and interest groups, and a new, better-educated politician. These new political actors are not satisfied with the old way of doing business and are trying to invent more productive politics for their countries. The public space that is growing, in however slow and halting a manner, holds the promise for more accountable and developmental governments that would use aid resources better. This prospect is just another reason it is so important for the West to nurture and protect this fledgling democratic space.

References

Acemoglu, Daron, Simon Johnson, and James Robinson. 2003. An African Success Story: Botswana. In *In Search of Prosperity: Analytical Narratives on Economic Growth*, ed. Dani Rodrik. Princeton, NJ: Princeton University Press.

Acharya, Arnab, Ana Fuzzo de Lima, and Mick Moore. 2003. The Proliferators: Transaction Costs and the Value of Aid. Institute of Development Studies, University of Sussex, Brighton, United Kingdom. Photocopy.

Adam, Christopher S., and Jan Willem Gunning. 2002. Redesigning the Aid Contract: Donors' Use of Performance Indicators in Uganda. *World Development* 30, no. 12: 2045–56.

Alesina, Alberto, and David Dollar. 2000. Who Gives Foreign Aid to Whom and Why? *Journal of Economic Growth* 5, no. 1: 33–63.

Alesina, Alberto, and Beatrice Weder. 2002. Do Corrupt Governments Receiveless Foreign Aid? *American Economic Review* 92, no. 4 (September): 1126–37.

Amsden, Alice. 1989. *Asia's Next Giant: South Korea and Late Industrialization*. New York: Oxford University Press.

Apedo Amah, Ayayi Togoata. 1997. Togo: Le Ventre Mou d'Une Démocratisation. In *L'Afrique Politique, 1997: Revendications Populaires et Recompositions Politiques*. Paris: Karthala.

Arndt, Channing. 2000. Technical Cooperation. In *Foreign Aid and Development: Lessons Learnt and Directions for the Future*, ed. Finn Tarp. London: Routledge.

Auty, R. M., ed. 2001. *Resource Abundance and Economic Development*. Oxford, UK: Oxford University Press.

Bandow, Doug, and Ian Vasquez. 1994. *Perpetuating Poverty: The World Bank, the IMF, and the Developing World*. Washington: CATO Books.

Banégas, Richard, and Patrick Quantin. 1996. Orientations et Limites de l'Aide Française au Développement Démocratique. *Revue Canadienne d'Etudes du Développement*, numéero spécial.

Bates, Robert H., and Paul Collier. 1993. The Politics and Economics of Economic Reform in Zambia. In *Political and Economic Interactions in Economic Policy Reform*, ed. Robert H. Bates and Anne Krueger. Oxford: Basil Blackwell.

Berg, Elliott. 1993. *Rethinking Technical Cooperation*. New York: United Nations Development Program.

Berg, Elliott. 1997. Dilemmas in Donor Aid Strategies. In *Perspectives on Aid and Development*, ed. Catherine Gwin and Joan M. Nelson. Washington: Overseas Development Council.

Berg, Elliott. 2000. Aid and Failed Reform: The Case of Public Sector Management. In *Foreign Aid and Development: Lessons Learnt and Directions for the Future*, ed. Finn Tarp. London: Routledge.

Bienen, Henry S., and Nicolas van de Walle. 1991. *Of Time and Power: Leadership Duration in the Modern World*. Stanford, CA: Stanford University Press.

Bierschenk, Thomas, and Jean Pierre Olivier de Sardan. 1997. Local Powers and a Distant State in Rural Central African Republic. *Journal of Modern African Studies* 35, no. 3 (September): 441–68.

Bingen, R. James. 1998. Cotton, Democracy, and Development in Mali. *Journal of Modern African Studies* 36, no. 2: 265–85.

Birdsall, Nancy, Stijn Claessens, and Ishac Diwan. 2001. *Will HIPC Matter? The Debt Game and Donor Behavior in Africa*. Carnegie Endowment for International Peace Economic Reform Project Discussion Paper 3. Washington: Carnegie Endowment for International Peace (March).

Birdsall, Nancy and Amar Hamoudi. 2002. *Commodity Dependence, Trade and Growth: When Openness Is Not Enough*. Center for Global Development Working Paper 7. Washington: Center for Global Development (May).

Birdsall, Nancy, and John Williamson. 2002. *Delivering on Debt Relief: From IMF Gold to a New Aid Architecture*. Washington: Institute for International Economics.

Blundo, Giorgio, and Jean Pierre Olivier de Sardan. 2001. La Corruption Quotidienne en Afrique de l'Ouest. *Politique Africaine*, no. 83 (October): 8–37.

Boone, Peter. 1996. Politics and the Effectiveness of Foreign Aid. *European Economic Review* 40, no. 2 (February): 289–329.

Booth, David. 2001. PRSP Institutionalization Study: PRSP Processes in 8 African Countries. Paper presented at the WIDER Development Conference on Debt Relief, Helsinki, August 17–18.

Bossuyt, Jean. 1997. La Participation des Acteurs Décentralisés et non Gouvernementaux. In *GEMDEV, La Convention de Lomé en Questions*. Paris: Karthala.

Boyce, James K. 2002. Unpacking Aid. *Development and Change* 33, no. 2: 239–46.

Brainard, Lael. 2003. Compassionate Conservatism Confronts Global Poverty. *The Washington Quarterly* 26, no. 2 (spring): 149–69.

Bratton, Michael. 1994. Micro Democracy? The Merger of Farmer Unions in Zimbabwe. *African Studies Review* 37, no. 1 (April): 9–37.

Bratton, Michael, and Nicolas van de Walle. 1997. *Democratic Experiments in Africa: Regime Transitions in Comparative Perspective*. New York: Cambridge University Press.

Bräutigam, Deborah. 1996. State Capacity and Effective Governance. In *Agenda for Africa's Economic Renewal*, ed. Benno Ndulu and Nicolas van de Walle. Washington: Overseas Development Council.

Bräutigam, Deborah. 2000. *Aid Dependence and Governance*. Stockholm: Almqvist and Wiksell International.

Burnell, Peter. 2001. Financial Indiscipline in Zambia's Third Republic: The Role of Parliamentary Scrutiny. *Journal of Legislative Studies* 7, no. 3 (autumn): 34–64.

Burnside, Craig, and David Dollar. 2000. Aid, Policies, and Growth. *American Economic Review* 90 (September): 847–68.

Campos, Ed, and Sanjay Pradhan. 1996. *Budgetary Institutions and Expenditure Outcomes: Binding Governments to Fiscal Performance*. World Bank Working Paper 1646. Public Economics Division, Policy Research Department. Washington: World Bank.

Carothers, Thomas. 1996. Aiding Post-Communist Societies: A Better Way? *Problems of Post-Communism* (September/October).

Cassen, Robert, & Associates. 1986. *Does Aid Work? Report to an Intergovernmental Task Force.* Oxford: Clarendon Press.

CDIE (Center for Development Information and Evaluation). 1998. *Democratic Decentralization in Mali: A Work in Progress.* CDIE Impact Evaluation 2. Washington: US Agency for International Development.

Chabal, Patrick. 2002. The Quest for Good Government and Development in Africa: Is NEPAD the Answer? *International Affairs* 78, no. 3: 567–83.

Chambers, Robert. 1983. *Rural Development: Putting the Last First.* New York: Longman.

Chipman, John. 1989. *French Power in Africa.* London: Blackwell.

Clark, John. 2003. *Worlds Apart: Civil Society and the Battle for Ethical Globalization.* Hartford, CT: Kumarian Press.

Clark, John. 1991. *Democratizing Development: The Role of Voluntary Organizations.* London: Earthscan.

Cohen, John. 1992. Foreign Advisors and Capacity Building: The Case of Kenya. *Public Administration and Development* 12: 493–510.

Collier, Paul. 1997. The Failure of Conditionality. In *Perspectives on Aid and Development,* ed. Catherine Gwin and Joan M. Nelson. Overseas Development Council Policy Essay 22. Baltimore, MD: Johns Hopkins University Press for the Overseas Development Council.

Collier, Paul, and David Dollar. 2000. Aid Allocation and Poverty Reduction. *European Economic Review* 46: 1475–500.

Collier, Paul, and Catherine Pattillo. 2000. *Reducing the Risk of Investment in Africa.* Basingstoke: Macmillan.

Cornia, Giovanni, Richard Jolly, and Frances Stewart. 1987. *Adjustment with a Human Face.* Oxford: Clarendon Press.

Cotton, Linda, and Vijaya Ramachandran. 2003. Governance and the Private Sector in Africa. In *Beyond Structural Adjustment: The Institutional Context of African Development,* ed. Nicolas van de Walle, Nicole Ball, and Vijaya Ramachandran. New York: Palgrave Macmillan.

Crozier, Michel, Samuel P. Huntington, and Joji Watanuki. 1975. *The Crisis of Democracy: Report on the Governability of Democracies to the Trilateral Commission.* New York: New York University Press.

Cummings, Gordon. 2000. Modernization Without "Banalisation": Towards a New Era in French-African Aid Relations. *Modern and Contemporary France* 8, no. 3: 359–70.

Dante, Idrissa, Jean François Gautier, Mohamed Ali Marouani, and Marc Raffinot. 2003. Mali. *Development Policy Review* 21, no. 2: 217–34.

Denning, Stephen. 1994. Programme Aid Beyond Structural Adjustment. Paper presented at a workshop on New Forms of Program Aid, Harare, Zimbabwe, January 31–February 1.

Development Initiatives. 2003. *Global Humanitarian Assistance.* Geneva: Development Initiatives.

Diamond, Larry. 2002. Thinking about Hybrid Regimes. *Journal of Democracy* 13, no. 2: 21–36.

Diamond, Larry. 1999. *Developing Democracy: Towards Consolidation.* Baltimore, MD: Johns Hopkins University Press.

Dicklitch, Susan. 1998. *The Elusive Promise of NGOs in Africa: Lessons from Uganda.* New York: St. Martin's Press.

Domingo, Pilar. 1999. Judicial Independence and Judicial Reform in Latin America. In *The Self-Restraining State: Power and Accountability in New Democracies,* ed. Andreas Schedler, Larry Diamond, and Marc Plattner. Boulder, CO: Lynne Rienner.

Easterly, William. 2003. The Cartel of Good Intentions: The Problem of Bureaucracy in Foreign Aid. *Policy Reform* 1: 1–28.

Easterly, William. 2001. *The Elusive Quest for Growth: Economists' Adventures and Misadventures in the Tropics.* Cambridge, MA: MIT Press.

Easterly, William, and Ross Levine. 1997. Africa's Growth Tragedy: Policies and Ethnic Divisions. *Quarterly Journal of Economics* 112 (November): 1203–250.

Easterly, William, Ross Levine, and David Roodman. 2003. *New Data, New Doubts: A Comment on Burnside and Dollar's "Aid, Policies, and Growth (2000)."* NBER Working Paper 9846. Cambridge, MA: National Bureau of Economic Research.

Eberlei, Walter. 2001. Insitutionalised Participation in Processes Beyond the PRSP. Study commissioned by the Deutsche Gesellschaft fur Technische Zusammenarbeit (GTZ) GmbH. Institute for Development and Peace, Gerhard-Mercator-University, Duisburg, Germany (September).

Eicher, Carl K. 2001. *Africa's Unfinished Business: Building Sustainable Agricultural Research Systems.* Michigan State University Department of Agricultural Economics Staff Paper 2001-10 (May 8). East Lansing, MI: Michigan State University.

Elbadawi, Ibrahim. 1996. Consolidating Macroeconomic Stabilization and Restoring Growth in Africa. In *Agenda for Africa's Economic Renewal*, ed. Benno Ndulu and Nicolas van de Walle. Washington: Overseas Development Council.

Emery, James. 2003. Governance and Private Investment in Africa. In *Beyond Structural Adjustment: The Institutional Context of African Development*, ed. Nicolas van de Walle, Nicole Ball, and Vijaya Ramachandran. New York: Palgrave Macmillan.

Emery, James, Melvin Spence, Timothy Buehrer, and Louis Wells. 2000. *Administrative Barriers to Foreign Investment: Reducing Red Tape in Africa.* Washington: World Bank.

Eriksson, John. 2001. *The Drive to Partnership: Aid Coordination and the World Bank.* Washington: World Bank.

Evans, Alison, and Erasto Ngalwea. 2003. Tanzania. *Development Policy Review* 21, no. 2: 271–87.

Evans, Peter B. 1995. *Embedded Autonomy: States and Industrial Transformation.* Princeton, NJ: Princeton University Press.

Fearon, James. 2002. Ethnic Structure and Cultural Diversity around the World: A Cross-National Data Set on Ethnic Groups. Paper presented at the annual meeting of the American Political Science Association, Boston, MA, August 29–September 3.

Ferroni, Marco, and Ashoka Mody, eds. 2002. *International Public Goods: Incentives, Measurement, and Financing.* Boston: Kluwer Academic Publishers.

Forman, Shepard, and Stewart Patrick, eds. 2002. *Good Intentions: Pledges of Aid for Postconflict Recovery.* Boulder, CO: Lynne Rienner.

Fox, Jonathan A., and L. David Brown, eds. 1998. *The Struggle for Accountability: The World Bank, NGOs, and Grassroots Movements.* Cambridge, MA: MIT Press.

Frisch, Dieter. 1997. La Dimension Politique dans les Rapports avec les Partenaires de Lomé. In *GEMDEV, La Convention de Lomé en Questions.* Paris: Karthala.

Frye, Timothy. 1997. A Politics of Institutional Choice: Post Communist Presidencies. *Comparative Political Studies* 30, no. 5 (October): 523–53.

Fukuda-Parr, Sakiko, Carlos Lopes, and Khalid Malik, eds. 2002. *Capacity for Development: New Solutions to Old Problems.* London: Earthscan.

Gallup, John, and Jeffrey Sachs. 1998. *Geography and Economic Development.* NBER Working Paper 6849 (December). Cambridge, MA: National Bureau of Economic Research.

Gelb, A. H. 1988. *Windfall Gain: Blessing or Curse?* New York: Oxford University Press.

Gerring, John, William Barndt, and Philip Bond. 2003. Democracy and Economic Growth: A Historical Perspective. Paper presented at the 2003 annual meeting of the American Political Science Association, Philadelphia, PA, August 27–September 1.

Goldsmith, Arthur A. 2003. Foreign Aid and State Administrative Capability. In *Beyond Structural Adjustment: The Institutional Context of African Development*, ed. Nicolas van de Walle, Nicole Ball, and Vijaya Ramachandran. New York: Palgrave Macmillan.

Goldsmith, Arthur A. 1999. Africa's Overgrown State Revisited: Bureaucracy and Economic Growth. *World Politics* 51, no. 4: 520–46.

Grindle, M. S., and M. E. Hildebrand. 1995. Building Sustainable Capacity in the Public Sector: What Can Be Done? *Public Administration and Development* 15: 441–63.

Gwin, Catherine, and Joan M. Nelson, eds. 1997. *Perspectives on Aid and Development*. Overseas Development Council Policy Essay 22. Baltimore, MD: Johns Hopkins University Press for the Overseas Development Council.

Haggard, Stephan, and Mathew McCubbins, eds. 2001. *Presidents, Parliaments, and Policy*. Cambridge University Press.

Harvey, Charles. 1992. Botswana: Is the Miracle Over? *Journal of African Economies* 1, no. 3 (November): 335–68.

Helleiner, Gerry. 2002. Local Ownership and Donor Performance Monitoring: New Aid Relationships in Tanzania? *Journal of Human Development* 3, no. 2: 251–61.

Hilhorst, Dorothea. 2003. *The Real World of NGOs*. New York: Palgrave.

Hulme, David, and Michael Edwards, eds. 1997. *NGOs, States, and Donors: Too Close for Comfort?* New York: St. Martin's Press.

Huntington, Samuel P. 1991. *The Third Wave: Democratization in the Late Twentieth Century*. Norman, OK: University of Oklahoma Press.

IDA and IMF (International Development Association and International Monetary Fund). 2002. Review of the Poverty Reduction Strategy Paper (PRSP) Approach: Main Findings. Washington: IDA and IMF (March 15).

IFIC and JICA (Institute for International Cooperation and Japan International Cooperation Agency). 2001. *Rethinking Poverty Reduction: PRSP and JICA*. Tokyo: IFIC/JICA (April).

IMF and IDA (International Monetary Fund and International Development Association). 2003. Poverty Reduction Strategy Papers: Detailed Analysis of Progress in Implementation. Washington: IMF and IDA (September 15).

Isham, Jonathan, Daniel Kaufmann, and Lant H. Pritchett. 1997. Civil Liberties, Democracy, and the Performance of Government Projects. *World Bank Economic Review* 11, no. 2 (May): 219–42.

Isham, Jonathan, Deepa Narayan, and Lant H. Pritchett. 1995. Does Participation Improve Performance? Establishing Causality with Subjective Data. *World Bank Economic Review* 9, no. 2 (May): 175–200.

Jenkins, Rob, and Maxton Tsoka. 2003. Malawi. *Development Policy Review* 21, no. 2: 197–215.

Jepma, Catrinus. 1994. *Inter-Nation Policy Coordination and Untying of Aid*. Aldershot: Ashgate Publishing.

Jepma, Catrinus. 1991. *The Tying of Aid*. Paris: Organization for Economic Cooperation and Development.

Jones, Stephen P. 1997. *Sector Investment Programs in Africa: Issues and Experience*. World Bank Technical Paper 374. Washington: World Bank.

Jones, Stephen, and Andrew Lawson. 2000. *Moving From Projects to Programmatic Aid*. OED Working Paper 5. Washington: World Bank.

Joseph, Richard. 1987. *Democracy and Prebendal Politics in Nigeria*. New York: Cambridge University Press.

Kanbur, Ravi, Todd Sandler, and Kevin Morrison. 1999. *The Future of Development Assistance: Common Pools and International Public Goods*. Policy Essay 25. Washington: Overseas Development Council.

Kapur, Devesh. 1997. The Weakness of Strength: The Challenge of Sub-Saharan Africa. In *The World Bank: Its First Half Century*, eds. Devesh Kapur, John P. Lewis, and Richard Webb. Washington: Brookings Institution Press.

Karatnycky, Adrian. 2004. The 2003 Freedom House Survey. *Journal of Democracy* 15, no. 1 (January): 82–93.

Kaufmann, Daniel. 2003. Governance Redux: The Empirical Challenge. Unpublished discussion paper. Washington: World Bank Institute (November 12).

Kaufmann, Daniel, Aart Kraay, and Pablo Zoido-Lobaton. 2002. *Governance Matters II: Updated Indicators for 2000–01*. World Bank Policy Research Department Working Paper 2772. Washington: World Bank.

Killick, Tony. 1998. *Aid and the Political Economy of Policy Change.* London: Routledge.

Kindleberger, Charles P. 1984. *Multinational Excursions.* Cambridge, MA: MIT Press.

Kirkpatrick, Jeanne J. 1982. *Dictatorships and Double Standards: Rationalism and Reason in Politics.* New York: Simon and Schuster.

Knack, Stephen. 2000. *Aid Dependence and the Quality of Governance.* World Bank Policy Research Working Paper 2396. Washington: World Bank.

Knack, Stephen, and Aminur Rahman. 2004. Donor Fragmentation and Bureaucratic Quality in Aid Recipients. Background paper. *World Development Report 2004.* Washington: World Bank.

Kumar, Krishna. 1997. *From Bullets to Ballots: Electoral Assistance to Postconflict Societies.* Washington: US Agency for International Development.

Lambright, Gina. 2003. The Dilemma of Decentralization: A Study of Local Politics in Uganda. PhD dissertation. Department of Political Science, Michigan State University.

Lancaster, Carol. 2000. *Transforming Foreign Aid: United States Assistance in the 21st Century.* Washington: Institute for International Economics.

Lancaster, Carol. 1999. *Aid to Africa: So Much to Do, So Little Done.* Chicago: University of Chicago Press.

Leftwich, A., ed. 1996. *Democracy and Development.* Cambridge, UK: Polity Press.

Lewis, Stephen R. 1993. Policy Making and Economic Performance: Botswana in Comparative Perspective. In *Botswana: The Political Economy of Democratic Development*, ed. Stephen John Stedman. Boulder, CO: Lynne Rienner Publishers.

LICUS Task Force. 2002. World Bank Group Work in Low-Income Countries Under Stress: A Task Force Report. World Bank, Washington. Photocopy (September).

Lienert, Ian, and Jitendra Modi. 1997. *A Decade of Civil Service Reform in Sub-Saharan Africa.* IMF Working Paper 97/179. Washington: International Monetary Fund.

Lienert, Ian, and Feridoun Sarraf. 2001. *Systemic Weaknesses of Budget Management in Anglophone Africa.* IMF Working Paper WP/01/211. Washington: International Monetary Fund (December).

Lindauer, David L., and Barbara Nunberg, eds. 1994. *Rehabilitating Government: Pay and Employment Reforms in Africa.* Washington: World Bank.

Linz, Juan J., and Arturo Valenzuela, eds. 1994. *The Failure of Presidential Democracy.* Baltimore, MD: Johns Hopkins University Press.

Lister, Stephen, ed. 1991. *Aid, Donors, and Development Management.* Windhoek, Namibia: Nepru Publications.

Lister, Stephen, and Mike Stevens. 1992. Aid Coordination and Management. World Bank, Washington. Photocopy (April 22).

Lucas, Robert E. 1988. On the Mechanics of Economic Development. *Journal of Monetary Economics* 22: 3–42.

Ludwig, Kimberly. 2001. *Prospects for Pluralism: Economic Interest Groups and Dual Transition in Zambia's Third Republic.* Dissertation, Michigan State University Department of Political Science.

Madavo, Callisto. 2002. African Perspectives on NEPAD: Talking Points. At the conference of African Ministers of Finance. Johannesburg, South Africa, October 19.

Mainwaring, Scott. 1993. Presidentialism, Multipartism, and Democracy: The Difficult Combination. *Comparative Political Studies* 26, no. 2 (July): 198–228.

Maipose, Gervase S., Gloria M. Somolekae, and Timothy A. Johnston. 1996. *Aid Effectiveness in Botswana.* Washington: Overseas Development Council.

Manor, James. 1999. *The Political Economy of Democratic Decentralization.* Washington: World Bank.

Martinussen, John Degnbol, and Poul Engberg-Pedersen. 1999. *Aid: Understanding International Development Cooperation.* New York: Palgrave.

Médard, Jean François. 1999. Les Avatars du Messianisme Francais en Afrique. In *L'Afrique Politique, 1999: Entre Transitions et Conflits.* Paris: Karthala.

Meyer, C. 1992. A Step Back as Donors Shift Institution Building from the Public to the Private Sector. *World Development* 20, no. 8: 1115–26.

Mosley, Paul, Jane Harrian, and J. F. L. Toye. 1995. *Aid and Power: The World Bank and Policy-Based Lending.* New York: Routledge.

Myers, C. Bernard. 2000. Budgetary Reform in Haiti from 1996-98: A Case Study of Issues and Obstacles in Implementing Change. *Public Budgeting and Finance* 20, no. 2 (summer): 74–90.

Ndegwa, Stephen. 2002. Decentralization in Africa: A Stocktaking Survey. Africa Region Working Paper (November).

Neumayer, Eric. 2002. Is Good Governance Rewarded? A Cross-National Analysis of Debt Forgiveness. *World Development* 30, no. 6: 913–30.

Nunberg, Barbara. 1997. *Rethinking Civil Service Reform: An Agenda for Smart Government.* Working Paper. Poverty and Social Policy Department, World Bank. Washington: World Bank.

OECD (Organization for Economic Cooperation and Development). 2004. Modest Increases in Development Aid in 2003. Press release, April 16. Paris: OECD.

OECD (Organization for Economic Cooperation and Development). 2002. Development Cooperation in Difficult Partnerships. Development Cooperation Directorate. DCD/ DAC(2002)11/REV1. Paris: OECD.

OECD (Organization for Economic Cooperation and Development). 1999. *Réformer les Systémes d'Aide: Le Cas du Mali.* Paris: OECD/UNDP/Club du Sahel.

Ottaway, Marina. 2002. Rebuilding State Institutions in Collapsed States. *Development and Change* 33, no. 5: 1001–123.

Oxfam. 2003. *Rigged Rules and Double Standards: Trade, Globalization, and the Fight Against Poverty.* Oxford, UK: Oxfam.

Powell, G. Bingham. 2000. *Elections as Instruments of Democracy: Majoritarian and Proportional Visions.* New Haven, CT: Yale University Press.

Prempeh, H. Kwasi. 1999. A New Jurisprudence for Africa. *Journal of Democracy* 19: 135–49.

Pritchett, Lant. 1997. Divergence, Big Time. *Journal of Economic Perspectives* 11, no. 3 (summer): 3–17.

Przeworski, Adam, Fernando Limongi, and Jose Antonio Cheibub. 2000. *Democracy and Development: Political Institutions and Well-Being in the World, 1950–1990.* New York: Cambridge University Press.

Przeworski, Adam, Susan C. Stokes, Bernard Manin, eds. 1999. *Democracy, Accountability, and Representation.* New York: Cambridge University Press.

Putnam, Robert D. 1992. *Making Democracy Work: Civic Traditions in Modern Italy.* Princeton, NJ: Princeton University Press.

Radelet, Steven. 2003. *Challenging Foreign Aid: A Policymaker's Guide to the Millennium Challenge Account.* Washington: Center for Global Development.

Rakner, Lise. 2003. *Political and Economic Liberalisation in Zambia, 1991–2001.* Stockholm: Nordiska Afrikainstitutet.

Rakner, Lise, Luke Mukubvu, Naomi Ngwira, and Kimberly Smiddy. 2004. The Budget as Theatre—Formal and Informal Institutional Makings of a Budget Process in Malawi. Christian Michelsen Institute, Bergen, Norway. Photocopy.

Razafindrakoto, Mireille, and François Roubaud. 1996. Ce qu'Attendent les Tananariviens de la Réforme de l'Etat et de l'Economie. *Politique Africaine* 61 (March): 54–72.

Reusse, Eberhard. 2002. *The Ills of Aid.* Chicago: University of Chicago Press.

Riddell, Roger C., and Mark Robinson. 1995. *Non-Governmental Organizations and Rural Poverty Alleviation.* Oxford: Clarendon Press.

Robinson, E. A. G., ed. 1960. *Economic Consequences of the Size of Nations.* New York: St. Martin's Press.

Ross, Michael. 1999. The Political Economy of the Resource Curse. *World Politics* 51, no. 2 (January): 297–322.

Sachs, Jeffrey. 2002. Weapons of Mass Salvation. *The Economist* (October 26, 2002).

Sachs, Jeffrey. 2001. The Strategic Significance of Global Inequality. *The Washington Quarterly* 24, no. 3 (summer).

Sachs, Jeffrey. 2000. *Tropical Underdevelopment.* CID Working Paper 57. Cambridge, MA: Center for International Development, Harvard University (December).

Sachs, Jeffrey, with Kwesi Botchwey, Maciej Cuchra, and Sara Sievers. 1999. *Implementing Debt Relief for the HIPCs.* Cambridge, MA: Center for International Development, Harvard University (August).

Schiavo-Campo, Salvatore, Giulio de Tommaso, and Amitabha Mukherjee. 1997. *Government Employment and Pay: A Global and Regional Perspective.* World Bank Policy Research Working Paper 1771. Washington: World Bank (May).

Schmidt, Steffen, James Scott, Laura Guasti, and Carl Landé, eds. 1977. *Friends, Followers, and Factions: A Reader in Political Clientelism.* Berkeley, CA: University of California Press.

Schwartz, Herman. 1999. A Brief History of Judicial Review. In *The Self-Restraining State: Power and Accountability in New Democracies,* ed. Andreas Schedler, Larry Diamond, and Marc Plattner. Boulder, CO: Lynne Rienner.

Shome, Parthasarathi. 1995. *Tax Policy Handbook.* Tax Policy Division, Fiscal Affairs Department. Washington: International Monetary Fund.

Simon, David. 2002. Aid and Democracy in Africa. Paper presented at the annual meeting of the American Political Science Association, San Francisco, August 30–September 2.

Smith, Zeric Kay. 2001. Mali's Decade of Democracy. *Journal of Democracy* 12, no. 3 (July): 70–79.

Stepan, Alfred, and Cindy Skach. 1993. Constitutional Frameworks and Democratic Consolidation: Parliamentarianism versus Presidentialism. *World Politics* 46 (October): 1–22.

Stern, Nicholas. 2003. Trade, Aid and Results: Can We Make a Difference? Keynote address to the Annual Bank Conference on Development Economics—Europe, May 15.

Stiglitz, Joseph E. 1996. *Economics of the Public Sector.* New York: W.W. Norton & Company.

Summers, Todd. 2003. *The Global Fund to Fight HIV/AIDS, TB, and Malaria: A Progress Report.* Washington: Center for Strategic and International Studies.

Svensson, Jakob. 1999. Aid, Growth, and Democracy. *Economics and Politics* 11, no. 3 (September): 275–97.

Tarp, Finn, ed. 2000. *Foreign Aid and Development: Lessons Learnt and Directions for the Future.* London: Routledge.

Tendler, Judith. 1997. *Good Government in the Tropics.* Baltimore: John Hopkins University Press.

Theobald, Robin. 1990. *Corruption, Development, and Underdevelopment.* London: Macmillan.

Therkildsen, Ole. 2001. Efficiency, Accountability, and Implementation: Public Sector Reform in East and Southern Africa. UNRISD, Democracy, Governance and Human Rights Programme Paper 3 (February).

Thiriot, Céline. 1999. Sur un Renouvellement Relatif des Elites au Mali. In *Le (Non-)Renouvellement des Elites en Afrique Subsaharienne,* ed. Jean-Pascal Daloz. Bordeaux: Centre d'Etude d'Afrique Noire.

Tidjani Alou, Mahaman S. 1998. La Décentralisation au Niger: Essai d'Approche. University of Niamey, Niger. Photocopy.

Tripp, Aili Mari. 2003. Forging Developmental Synergies Between States and Associations in Africa. In *Beyond Structural Adjustment: The Institutional Context of African Development,* ed. Nicolas van de Walle, Nicole Ball, and Vijaya Ramachandran. New York: Palgrave Macmillan.

UNCTAD (United Nations Conference on Trade and Development). 2002. *The Least Developed Countries Report 2002: Escaping the Poverty Trap.* Geneva: UNCTAD.

USAID (US Agency for International Development). 2003. Uzbekistan Country Profile. www.usaid.gov.country/ee.uz/.

Uvin, Peter. 1998. *Aiding Violence: The Development Enterprise in Rwanda*. West Hartford, CT: Kumarian Press.

van de Walle, Nicolas. 2002. Elections Without Democracy: Africa's Range of Regimes. *Journal of Democracy* 13, no. 2 (April): 66–80.

van de Walle, Nicolas. 2001. *African Economies and the Politics of Permanent Crisis, 1979-1999*. New York: Cambridge University Press.

van de Walle, Nicolas. 1993. The Politics of Non-Reform in Cameroon. In *Hemmed in: Responses to Africa's Economic Decline*, ed. Thomas Callaghy and John Ravenhill. New York: Columbia University Press.

van de Walle, Nicolas, and Timothy Johnston. 1996. *Improving Aid to Africa*. Baltimore, MD: Johns Hopkins University Press for the Overseas Development Council.

Van Rooy, Alison, ed. 1998. *Civil Society and the Aid Industry*. London: Earthscan Publications.

Vengroff, Richard. 1993. Democratic Governance and the Party System in Mali. *Journal of Modern African Studies* 31, no. 4: 541–62.

Wade, Robert. 2001. The US Role in the Malaise at the World Bank: Get up Gulliver. Photocopy. Paper for G24 Dicussion Paper Series. Washington: Intergovernmental Group of Twenty-Four.

Wade, Robert. 1990. *Governing the Market: Economic Theory and the Role of Government in East Asian Industrialization*. Princeton, NJ: Princeton University Press.

White, Howard. 1998. *Aid and Macro-Economic Performance*. Basingstoke: Macmillan.

White, Howard. 1996. How Much Aid is Used for Poverty Reduction? *IDS Bulletin* 27, no. 1.

White, Howard, and Geske Dijkstra. 2003. *Programme Aid and Development: Beyond Conditionality*. London and New York: Routledge.

Whittington, Dale, and Craig Calhoun. 1988. Who Really Wants Donor Coordination? *Development Policy Review* 6, no. 3: 295–309.

Whittle, Dennis. 2002. International Development: Imagining a New Paradigm. Photocopy (August). Presentation to the Center for Global Development, Washington.

Widner, Jennifer. 1999. Building Judicial Independence in Common Law Africa. In *The Self-Restraining State: Power and Accountability in New Democracies*, ed. Andreas Schedler, Larry Diamond, and Marc Plattner. Boulder, CO: Lynne Rienner.

Williamson, John. 1993. Democracy and the "Washington Consensus." *World Development* 21, no. 8: 1329–36.

World Bank. 2003a. *Toward Country-Led Development: A Multi-Partner Evaluation of the Comprehensive Development Framework*. Washington: World Bank.

World Bank. 2003b. *World Development Report 2003*. Washington: World Bank.

World Bank. 2002a. *The Role and Effectiveness of Development Assistance: Lessons from World Bank Experience*. Development Economics Vice Presidency, World Bank.

World Bank. 2002b. *Haiti: Country Assistance Evaluation*. Report 23637 (February 12). Washington: World Bank.

World Bank. 2002c. *Pakistan: Development Policy Review*. Report 23916-PAK (April 3). Washington: World Bank.

World Bank. 2001a. *Zambia: Public Expenditure Review*. Report 22543-ZA (December). Washington: World Bank.

World Bank. 2001b. *Adjustment Lending Retrospective*. Washington: World Bank (June 15).

World Bank. 2000. *World Development Report 2000*. Washington: World Bank.

World Bank. 1998. *Assessing Aid: What Works, What Doesn't and Why*. New York: Oxford University Press for the World Bank.

World Bank. 1997. *World Development Report 1997*. New York: Oxford University Press.

World Bank. 1986. *Structural Adjustment Lending: A First Review of Experience*. Operations Evaluation Report 6409 (September 24). Washington: World Bank.

Young, Crawford, and Thomas Turner. 1985. *The Rise and Decline of the Zairian State*. Madison, WI: University of Wisconsin Press.

Index

accountability, 35, 77
 horizontal
  engendered by democratization, 85
  of governments, 74
  low level of, 26
 vertical, 26, 73–74, 85
Afghanistan, 7n
African, Caribbean, and Pacific (ACP) states, 68
African Growth and Opportunity Act (AGOA), 97
aid. See foreign aid
Akayev, Askar, 17
Angola, 7n, 8
Aristide, Jean-Bertrand, 18
Armenia, 11
authoritarian regimes, 13, 84, 87. See also hybrid political systems

Bangladesh, 8n
Benin, 8n
Botswana, 69–70
brain drain, 99
Brazil, 22
British Department for International Development (DFID), 43
budgetary oversight, impact of inadequate resources on, 16
bureaucracies, 92. See also civil service
 attachment to a given volume of aid, 89
 politics in donor agencies , 75–77
 rent-seeking, associated with foreign aid, 71
Burkina Faso, 8n, 61
Burundi, 7n
Bush, George W., 3–4

Cambodia, 8n
Cameroon, 11, 45
capacity building
 capacity utilization approach, 95
 civil service and, 96–97
 government economic planning and, 95–96
 local approach, 93
 "projectization" of, 72
capital flight, discouraging, 98
CAS. See country assistance strategy
Central African Republic
 compared with Gabon, 30, 30n
 democratic transition, 13
 economic characteristics, 9t
 international economic links, 31t
 as a military government, 86
 political longevity, 12t
central state. See also decentralization
 bypassing, 57–63
 as the key player, 36
Chad
 economic characteristics, 9t
 international economic links, 31t
 not excluded as war-torn, 7n
 oil resources, 30
 political longevity, 12t
Chiluba, Frederick, 27
China, 23
civil service
 budgets, underfunded for, 25
 capacity building and , 96–97
 capacity declining over time, 73
 progressive erosion of salaries, 24–25
 promotions for, 25
 public employment in, 25f

resisting political conditionality or selectivity, 86–87
rewarding governments doing the right thing, 89
selecting recipients of foreign aid, 40
tension between ownership and selectivity objectives, 67–69
transparency, 92
unchanging incentives of, 74–78
undoing positive effects of other donors, 47
viewing institutional capacity as a given, 72–73
economic development. *See* development
economic instability, 70
economic performance, 7
economic planning, 95–96
economic stability, 82–84
economies
    identified as low-income, 7
    inability of the poorest to grow, 1
    war-torn, 7–8
Egypt, 46
electoral politics, 13
    direct elections, 14
    multiparty elections, 13
    single-party regime, death of, 13
Eritrea, 7*n*
Ethiopia, 7, 7*n*
ethnic fractionalization, 29, 29*n*
European aid, 68
European Commission, 68
European Union, 90
executive branch, 14, 19
expenditure management, 73–74
Eyadema, Gnassingbe, 13, 18

FDI. *See* foreign direct investment
foreign aid
    allocation of, 74–75
    benefits of, 37
    contradictions of current doctrine, 37–63
    coordination, 46–47, 96
    crisis of faith about, 2
    cutting off military governments' access to, 86
    dependence, 38
    expenditures, 92
    failure of traditional conditionality, 37
    focusing on the neediest, 43
    focus of agencies, 88
    goals not achieved, 36
    government management of, 47
    implementation of programs, 75, 76
    least effective in poorest countries, 37
    maintaining control over implementation, 76
    modalities, 76
    motivations for, 44
    performance-based allocation of aid resources, 81

policies, 97–100
political climate for increasing, 3
poverty trap justifying, 4
process, 69
program aid, failure to move to, 76
project and program funding, incentives to spend, 75
project proliferation, 67
project structure, 76
promoting economic development, 1
recipient distribution by the number of donors, 48
recipients, 46
reduction implied by selectivity, 40
reform, 65–78
required for further development, 34–35
resources, 81
role in the struggle against terrorism, 44
in stagnant low-income states, 31*t*, 33–36
success of, 2
transaction costs of foreign aid projects, 48
triggers for cutting off, 88
foreign direct investment (FDI), 32
foreign experts
    curtailing reliance on, 95
    determining the number of, 49
    donor preference for long-term, 71–72
    predilection for, 76
France, 44, 47
Freedom House survey, 11

Gabon, 30, 30*n*
Gambia, The
    Alliance for Patriotic Reorientation and Construction (APRC), 17
    budgetary auditing function, 16
    economic characteristics, 9*t*
    international economic links, 31*t*
    political longevity, 12*t*
    political system, 13, 13*n*
geostrategic pressures, 88
Ghana
    civil service reform, 96–97
    economic characteristics, 9*t*
    international economic links, 31*t*
    jurisprudence of executive supremacy, 17
    political liberalization, 87
    political longevity, 12*t*
    program aid, 76
    sector program for health, 52
Global Fund to Fight HIV/AIDS, Tuberculosis, and Malaria, 3
global public goods, 89, 99
governance
    improvements, 84
    indicators, 22–23
government
    capacity, 72
    at the center of the development process, 69

government *(Cont.)*
  coordination, 69
  cutting off assistance to military, 86
  development activities, 51
  economic planning, 95–96
  encouraging proactive, 70
  foreign aid sustaining nondevelopmental, 37
  integrating foreign aid into programs, 51
  local, 60–63
  management of aid, 47
  ownership of aid activities, 49, 50–51, 56
  predatory behavior of officials, 22
  proactive, 70
  technocratic component of, 26
Guinea
  constitutional change allowing an additional term, 18
  economic characteristics, 9*t*
  international economic links, 31*t*
  political longevity, 12*t*
  political system, 11
Guinea-Bissau
  democratic transition, 13
  economic characteristics, 9*t*
  international economic links, 31*t*
  political longevity, 12*t*

Haiti, 11, 73
heavily indebted poorest countries (HIPC) debt initiative, 45, 52
HIV/AIDS
  as global crisis, 2
  Global Fund to Fight HIV/AIDS, Tuberculosis, and Malaria, 3
  research on, 100
human development, low, 29
hybrid political systems, 11–14

IFIs. *See* international financial institutions (IFIs)
illiteracy rate. *See also* literacy rates
  female, 9*t*
IMF. *See* International Monetary Fund
import-substitution industrialization (ISI) policies, 29
incentives
  creating the right, 80–81
  improving for development, 89–93
  unchanging for donors, 74–78
independent service authorities (ISAs), 80
India, 8*n*
instability. *See* economic instability
institutional capacity
  elusiveness of, 70–74
  incentives for governments to increase, 93
  not improving, 23–24
  viewed as a given by donors, 72–73
integrated financial management information systems (IFMIS), 73

interest groups, 26, 27
international financial institutions (IFIs)
  aid based on quality of macroeconomic policies, 42
  loans to military governments, 86
  PRSPs and, 52
  transferring tasks to regional institutions, 99
  undermining conditionality requirements of, 47
International Monetary Fund (IMF), 52
international trade, 32
Ireland, 28

Japan, 53
judicial branch, 17

Kaunda, Kenneth, 20, 27
Kenya
  economic characteristics, 9*t*
  international economic links, 31*t*
  local government tax collection, 62
  political longevity, 12*t*
  salary of a mid-level economist, 25
  term limits introduced, 18
Khama, Seretse, 87
Konaré, Alpha Oumar, 11, 19
Korea, 22
Kyrgyzstan
  Askar Akayev and, 17
  economic characteristics, 9*t*
  foreign aid received, 41
  international economic links, 31*t*
  political longevity in, 12*t*
  political system of, 11

Laos, 8*n*
leaders, reform role of exceptional, 80–81
legal systems, antiquated, 17
legislatures, 14, 16
liberal political reform, 84
Liberia, 7*n*, 86–87
LICUS. *See* Low Income Countries Under Stress group
literacy rates, 9*t*, 29
local expertise in managerial and technical skills, 94
local model, adopting, 93–95
local ownership, 37, 48, 91. *See also* ownership of aid activities
local populations, improving project performance, 49
local revenues, absence of, 62
local wage scale, distorted, 94
low-income countries. *See* stagnant low-income states (SLIS)
Low Income Countries Under Stress (LICUS) group, 79–80

Madagascar
democratic transition, 13
economic characteristics, 9t
election loss by a standing president, 18
international economic links, 31t
mistrust of public officials, 22
political longevity, 12t
malaria, 29. *See also* tropical diseases
Malawi
budgetary auditing function, 16
democratic transition, 13
economic characteristics, 9t
inadequate funding for the parliament, 16
international economic links, 31t
political longevity, 12t
PRSP participatory processes and
government accountability, 56
Mali
arrondissements replaced by communes,
61
democratic governments, 43
democratic transition, 13
economic characteristics, 9t
evolution toward liberal democracy, 19
foreign aid received, 41
international economic links, 31t
OECD report on foreign aid in, 48
political longevity, 12t
political system, 11
president's party not the biggest single
party, 17
progression away from presidentialism, 19
SYCOV organization of cotton farmers, 28
term limits introduced, 18
Mauritania
economic characteristics, 9t
international economic links, 31t
political longevity, 12t
Mauritius, 25
Mbeki, Thabo, 46
MCA. *See* Millennium Challenge Account
MDGs. *See* Millennium Development Goals
military governments, cutting off donor
assistance to, 86
Millennium Challenge Account (MCA), 3, 45
Millennium Declaration, 3
Millennium Development Goals (MDGs), 3
Mobutu Sese Seko, 21
Moi, Daniel Arap, 18
Moldova
Communist Party of Moldova (PCM), 17
economic characteristics, 9t
from Europe and Central Asia, 8
foreign aid received, 33
international economic links, 31t
political longevity, 12t
Mongolia
economic characteristics, 9t
governance ranking, 23
international economic links, 31t

Mongolian People's Revolutionary Party
(MPRP), 17
political longevity, 12t
Mozambique, 8n
Mugabe, Robert, 17
multilateral lending, 41
Myanmar, 8n

nation building, 8
natural resources, 30
Nepal, 8n
New Economic Partnership for Africa's
Development (NEPAD), 2, 46
NGOs. *See* nongovernmental organizations
Nicaragua
economic characteristics, 9t
international economic links, 31t
political longevity, 12t
Niger
decentralization program, 61
democratic transition, 13
economic characteristics, 9t
international economic links, 31t
political longevity, 12t
Nigeria
economic characteristics, 9t
economy, 28
FDI in, 32
international economic links, 31t
oil, 30
political longevity, 12t
nongovernmental organizations (NGOs)
adversarial spirit of government relations,
66
as a complement to the central state, 36
continuing independent project type of
assistance, 78
corruption and fraud by, 60
dependence on donors, 59–60
emergence of, 59–60
implementing projects with local, 94
improving performance of aid projects, 49
low absorptive capacity of, 59
in the low-income economies, 59
PRSP presentations to, 56
sustainability problems of
NGO-implemented aid, 60, 66–67
weakest in the countryside, 28
in the Western community, 100–101
nonstate actors, 26–28

official development assistance (ODA)
accepting a lower volume of, 89
evaluation of, 41
increases in, 3
received by stagnant low-income states,
31t, 33–34, 33f, 34t
top three donors of gross, 54–55

Organization for Economic Cooperation and
    Development (OECD)
  Development Assistance Committee (DAC),
    92
  report on foreign aid in Mali, 48
ownership
  donor rhetoric on, 50
  promoted by PRSPs, 56
  promoting, 49, 50–51
  versus selectivity, 67–69

Pakistan
  decentralization process, 61
  economic characteristics, 9*t*
  economy, 28
  international economic links, 31*t*
  as a key ally in the struggle against
    terrorism, 88
  as a military government, 86
  political longevity, 12*t*
  political system, 11, 13, 13*n*
parliamentary systems, 14–15, 15*t*
participatory processes, 56
  decision making, 52
patronage, 20, 21
peace, benefit to low-income countries of,
    8
peasant society, clientelism in, 20
planning. *See* economic planning
political and institutional change, 35–36
political characteristics of stagnant low-income
    states, 11–28
political clientelism, 19–23
political conditionality, 85, 86–87
political governance issues, 42
political liberalization, 75
political longevity, 12*t*
political participation, 84
political parties, 16
political reform, 13
political selectivity, 85–87
"poor but virtuous" country, 42
poorest countries, core set of, 2
population
  smallness of, 29
  of stagnant low-income states, 9*t*
poverty
  alleviation, 43
  headcount, 9*t*
  level, 29
Poverty Reduction and Growth Facility
    (PRGF) loans, 52
Poverty Reduction Strategy Papers (PRSP)
    approach, 51
  budgetary process and, 68
  designed with a common pool logic, 82
  documents and policies defined by the
    World Bank, 57
  economic planning and, 96
  implementation as donor-driven, 67

implementation of donor projects in
    support of, 57
  inability to arrest fragmentation, 53
  ownership promoted by, 56
  participatory process required by, 56, 67
  rarely formally debated in the national
    legislature, 68
  scope and substantive focus of, 57
  focus on service delivery, 57
"poverty trap", 4, 7
power
  alternation of, 18–19, 87
  personalization of, 19
prebendalism, 20–21, 22
presidents
  longevity in office, 17–19, 87
  politics, revolving around, 17
presidentialism, 14–19, 85
PRGF loans. *See* Poverty Reduction and
    Growth Facility loans
private Americans, donations to Third World
    countries, 59
private investment, facilitating, 97
private sector, 59, 97–99
procurement
  generated by donor projects, 48
  in Haiti, 73
protectionism, curtailing Western, 98–99
PRSP approach. *See* Poverty Reduction
    Strategy Papers approach
public goods and services, 58, 89, 99
public sector
  employment. *See* civil service
  public expenditure reviews (PERS), 73
  institutions, 23–26
  public investment program (PIP), 73
  management programs, 72
  versus private, 59

Ramgoolam, Seewoosagur, 87
Ratsiraka, Didier, 18
Ravalomanana, Marc, 18
Rawlings, Jerry, 87
reform mongering, 74
reforms, creating the right incentives for,
    80–81
regional institutions, 99–100
relief operations, NGOs as dominant players, 59
rent-seeking
  aid system providing a cover for, 47
  associated with foreign aid, 71
  linked to prebendalism, 22
Republic of the Congo, 11
Romania, 94
Rural Producers' Organization project, 28*n*
Rwanda, 7*n*, 86

salaries
  paid by donor projects, 49
  progressive erosion of civil service, 24–25